3-5-79

HANDS-ON BASIC WITH A PET

HANDS-ON BASIC WITH A PET

Herbert D. Peckham
Professor of Natural Science
Gavilan College

McGraw-Hill Book Company

New York   St. Louis   San Francisco   Auckland   Bogota   Dusseldorf
Johannesburg   London   Madrid   Mexico   Montreal   New Delhi
Panama   Paris   Sao Paulo   Singapore   Sydney   Tokyo   Toronto

HANDS-ON BASIC WITH A PET

1234567890 DODO 783210987

This book was set in Megaron by Instant Type, Monterey, California. The editors were Charles Stewart and Annette Hall. The cover photograph is courtesy of Commodore Business Machines. The production supervisor was Rich Ausburn. R. R. Donnelley was printer and binder.

Library of Congress Cataloging in Publication Data

Peckham, Herbert D
  Hands-on BASIC with a PET.

  Includes index.
  1. Basic (Computer program language)
2. PET (Computer) — Programming. I. Title.
QA76.73.B3P42   001.6'424   78-21858
ISBN 0-07-049157-7

TABLE OF CONTENTS

2041014

PREFACE

This book is a modification of an earlier work by the author also published by McGraw-Hill Book Company. The book, titled "BASIC: A Hands-On Method," introduces students to BASIC on a number of different timesharing computers. This earlier material has been revised and modified to be used specifically on the PET personal computer manufactured by Commodore Business Machines in Palo Alto, California. Since the motivation and ideas that lead to the original work are equally valid with regard to the PET, they bear repeating in this book.

Two characteristics of most BASIC programming texts on the market are very objectionable. First, almost all quickly begin to use mathematics at a level that excludes the vast majority of the people we are most interested in, many of whom can rely on introductory algebra (very dimly remembered) but who, for a variety of reasons, want to learn how to program in BASIC. The second objection is that generally nothing in the structure of most BASIC texts requires the beginner to spend much (if any) time on the computer. Students typically try to study programming like any other subject and do not feel the need to experiment with and execute programs on the computer. It seems axiomatic that much more effective learning will take place if most of the study of BASIC utilizes the computer. This text's main thesis is that more traditional text material should be preceded by a good deal of time experimenting with the language on the computer. The experience to date validates the idea that students work though the material more rapidly and effectively with this initial exposure to BASIC on the computer.

Most textbooks are used in a classroom environment as part of the formal educational system. Certainly, many students will learn how to program the PET in this traditional setting. However, the sales of personal computers like PET touch all parts of our society. This means that the usual concept of a "student" must be changed dramatically. This text has been designed to be useful to anyone (whether part of the educational system or not) who wants to learn how to program the PET in BASIC.

The reader will immediately note that the book is structured quite differently from most programming texts. Each chapter begins with a statement of the objectives for that chapter. Then the student is guided through a set of exercises that demonstrates BASIC in action and permits experimentation with its characteristics. Once a "feel" for BASIC has been acquired, one can more profitably proceed to the usual text treatment. The mathematics level has intentionally been kept very low. The student with more advanced mathematical skills will have little difficulty learning how to employ these skills on the PET. However, if the mathematics level in the text were set too high, the majority of beginners would become discouraged in the first few chapters. At the level presented, nearly anyone should be able to work through the material without getting "hung up" by the mathematics. The student must have access to a PET to use this text.

The text is organized into ten chapters. If used in a classroom setting, each chapter forms a block of instruction that should require about two hours of classroom time and possibly three or four hours of time outside class. Review tests are provided at the end of each chapter, enabling the student to see if the objectives have been mastered.

The text can be used in several different ways. First, and probably most important, it can be used with no supervision as a self-study text. It has also been used in an open-entry, open-exit, self-paced course. If desired, the material can be presented in a traditional lecture format.

Students at any level, from junior high through graduate school, from housewife to senior citizen, from factory worker to professional, should be able to use the material without difficulty. The goal is to provide programming skills in BASIC as rapidly and effectively as possible. Because of the level of the presentation, no attempt has been made to utilize all the capabilities of PET, some of which are very sophisticated. As indicated above, no mathematics past introductory algebra is required, and the algebra used is mainly formula evaluation. More mathematical ability is nice but unnecessary.

Acknowledgments

Particular thanks are due Mr. Hugh Getty, Vice President of Marketing of Commodore Business Machines, for the valuable assistance he provided. The name PET is a registered trademark with regard to any computer product, and is owned by Commodore Business Machines, a division of Commodore International. Permission to use the trademark name PET in this book has been granted by Commodore Business Machines, and is gratefully acknowledged. The author is also grateful for much useful information obtained from the PET User's Group Newsletter published at the Lawrence Hall of Science, University of California at Berkeley. The errors that remain are, or course, due to me.

Comments or suggestions for improvement of this book will be appreciated.

Herbert D. Peckham

HANDS-ON BASIC WITH A PET

THE PET COMPUTER AND BASIC

Computers are now a common part of our lives. We may not see them, but they are there, involved in some way in most of our daily activities. Business of all sizes, educational institutions, various branches of government—none would be able to handle the bewildering quantity of information that seems to characterize our society without using computers. Only recently, however, has it been possible to bring small, inexpensive computers into the home or classroom. For the first time, people in all walks of life, from students to senior citizens, are becoming involved with computers. As the price of computers continues to drop, this trend will surely go on. More and more people will want to know how to use computers to enable them to participate fully in our society.

1-1 WHAT IS BASIC?

You are about to embark upon the study of a computer language called BASIC using a very powerful home computer called PET. PET stands for "Personal Electronic Transactor." BASIC is a very specialized language designed to permit you and the computer to understand and communicate with one another. This language is certainly much easier to use than a spoken language such as Spanish or French. Even so, BASIC does have a simple vocabulary consisting of a few words, a grammatical structure, and rules of usage just like any other language. The first task will be to learn the vocabulary of BASIC and become used to its rules of grammar. Next, we will see how the language permits you to use the computer in a wide range of activities. The level of mathematics involved has intentionally been kept very low. Therefore, if you feel a bit rusty in your mathematical skills, don't be too concerned. As we proceed through BASIC, you will have an opportunity to brush up on some elementary mathematics.

A very effective way to learn is to observe details and characteristics while actually performing a task: the "discovery" method. This is the strategy that will be used in this book. You will be asked to begin each chapter with a discovery session on the PET. After following the directions and watching closely what the computer does in response to your instructions, you will begin to acquire a "feel" for BASIC and how the PET operates. Once you have this type of understanding, you can proceed more profitably to study the written material that summarizes what you have learned. Thus, the directed exercise on the PET is a key part of learning about BASIC as presented in this book.

1

1-2 WHERE DID BASIC ORIGINATE?

The original version of BASIC was designed and written at Dartmouth College under the direction of Professors John G. Kemeny and Thomas E. Kurtz. In September 1963, work began on the concept of time sharing on a computer and the creation of a programming language written from a user's point of view. A very interesting sidelight is that much of the actual programming on the project was done by undergraduate students at Dartmouth. The birthday of BASIC is May 1, 1964, so the language is still a teen ager.

The success of this pioneering effort at Dartmouth soon attracted national attention, and very quickly other institutions became interested. The rest is history. Today, nearly every time-sharing computer supports the BASIC language. The most recent development is the implementation of BASIC on small home computers like the PET. Each year, the percentage of total computer activities done in BASIC increases. What started as a project at a single college is now an established part of the computer industry throughout the world.

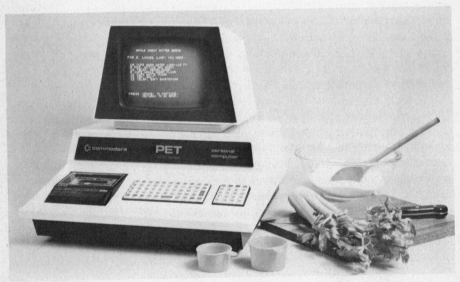

(Photograph courtesy of Commodore Business Machines.)

1-3 WHAT IS PET?

The concept of a powerful computer, comparable in size and price with a color television set, capable of doing most if not all the tasks that formerly required large computers in air-conditioned isolation, is a new and somewhat unsettling idea. However unsettling the concept may be, this is precisely what has happened. PET, produced by Commodore Business Machines in Palo Alto, California, is one of the first of the "personal computers" that have exploded onto the marketplace.

Before getting into how to program in BASIC on the PET we should pause to examine the origins of PET, and point out some of its remarkable characteristics. Above all else, two things are important about the PET. First, the price is such that large numbers of people will either own a PET or have access to one. This raises the second point that needs to be emphasized. The question of accessibility to computer facilities has always been difficult to deal with. Often, it seemed that barriers, some real and some imaginary, were placed in the paths of those who desired to use computers. With the PET, all such barriers are gone. Thus, PET is found in homes, offices, and classrooms across the country. By definition, "personal computing" has to be "accessible computing," and the PET provides it!

The heart of PET is a microcomputer on a chip. The first such microcomputers were manufactured in 1973, so a very new technology is involved. From the very beginning, Commodore believed in the concept of personal computing and created the PET with several distinct and important goals in mind. The first is the ability to have a graphic display—or stated simply, PET should be able to draw pictures. This is important since it is much easier to communicate with others through pictures and graphs than through numbers and equations. Second, it was clear that BASIC would be the language of PET, and that it would have to be powerful enough to permit a wide range of uses from the novice playing games to the professional programmer. BASIC was selected because of good earlier experience with time-sharing computers. BASIC is a "friendly" and nonthreatening language that is easy to learn but has powerful capabilities. In short, it is ideal for personal computing and has been almost universally adopted for personal computers.

It is startling to learn that PET moved from conception to a working prototype in only eight weeks! In most areas of manufacturing, such a short development time would be out of the ordinary indeed! However, the one thing that seems to characterize the dynamic new semiconductor industry is rapid change. New developments, such as PET, become the norm rather than the exception. So, the user of personal computers must become accustomed to rapid, exciting, and dynamic change. However rapid the change, nothing should detract from the exciting new opportunities and vistas provided by PET. Literally, PET has to be seen to be believed, and one quickly discovers that PET is its own best salesperson.

1-4 HOW TO BEGIN

You should approach each chapter in the book in the same way. The material has been organized with special learning patterns in mind, and any change will be less effective and require more of your time.

Each chapter begins with a brief statement of the objectives. These should be studied carefully in order for you to get a clear picture of precisely what is to be done. (It's nice to know where you're going!) When asked, you should record the computer output in the space provided. Occasionally you will be asked to answer questions. The purpose of this activity is to lead you through the ideas involved and let you see BASIC working. It is important that you try to think about what will happen in situations that will be set up. Quite often you will be deliberately led into error situations. The purpose, of course, is to draw you into the meat of programming! This is an active relationship between you and your PET that should not be slighted. Time spent in this activity will save you much more time later on.

Following the discovery exercises in each chapter, a complete discussion is given to cover all the objectives a second time. Since you will have already seen the ideas and concepts in action on the computer, your study of this material will be much easier and profitable.

Typical programs are included in each chapter. These are discussed in great detail to point out how the parts are pulled together to produce a BASIC program. Of course, the ultimate goal in all the chapters is to learn how to write and execute BASIC programs on the PET. Thus, be sure to allow sufficient time to study and understand all the examples.

Each chapter after Chapter 4 has a collection of problems. You should plan to work enough problems to satisfy yourself that you can write programs at the level appropriate to that chapter. Solutions to the odd-numbered problems are given at the end of the book.

Finally, each chapter (except the first) has a practice test. The purpose of this test is to review your understanding of the material and point out any areas that need further study. The answers to the practice tests are in a section at the end of the book.

One final comment: it is very easy to become pompous about programming, even with such an enchanting computer as PET. Programming texts tend to be as dry as popcorn. Since most students soon discover that learning to program in BASIC is good fun, we may as well relax. In this spirit, cartoons ("Herb's Blurbs") will be included from time to time for your enjoyment.

GETTING ACQUAINTED WITH THE PET

Since your first contact with the PET may seem a bit strange and complicated, we will proceed very slowly. Rest assured that after a few sessions using the PET, routine operations will seem very natural and will cause you no trouble. Initially, though, be prepared for a certain "confusion quotient."

2-1 OBJECTIVES

In this chapter we want to get familiar with the PET and start learning how it operates. No BASIC programming will be done until the next chapter. However, learning how the PET keyboard operates, and how information is entered and modified, is fundamental to all that will follow. This material is very easy to master, but do make sure that you understand all the objectives thoroughly.

Calculator Mode

One of the easiest ways to use the PET is as a simple calculator. Of course, if this was all PET could do, it would be a very expensive calculator! In due time we will learn how to do much more indeed, but for the present, simple arithmetic operations in the calculator mode are a nice introduction to operation of the PET.

Screen Editing

Rarely can information be entered into a computer without making mistakes. The PET has a screen editing feature that makes it possible to easily change or correct material that has been entered. A thorough knowledge of this feature will save you a great deal of time later on.

Screen Graphics

As pointed out in the first chapter, the PET has built-in graphic capabilities that are very powerful. Using these capabilities, diagrams, charts, and pictures can be created on the screen. When complicated graphics are woven into BASIC programs, the techniques are nontrivial and might be very confusing for the beginner. We will, however, explore some of the simpler graphic capabilities which will introduce you to the topic.

2-2 DISCOVERY ACTIVITIES

Before beginning work on the PET, we must establish several important points. On a typewriter, a lower-case L is used for the numeral 1. A different key is used, however, on the PET. The numeral 1 is found with the other numeral keys at the right side of the keyboard. One of the most frequent mistakes made by the beginner is to type L when the numeral 1 is desired. Next, don't use the upper case O for the numeral 0. Like the numeral 1, the 0 on the PET keyboard is found with the numeral keys. Also note that the zero has a slash through it to distinguish it from the letter O.

Don't use the L for the 1!

Don't use the Oh for the 0!

Take a few minutes to examine the PET keyboard. Note that with the exception of the red SHIFT, SPACE, and RETURN keys, all the keys have upper and lower functions. If you want the lower function, simply press the key. If you want the upper function, you must hold the red SHIFT key down while pressing the desired key. Of course, this is precisely the same as the shift key on a typewriter.

Now we are ready to begin working on the PET. Sit down in front of the PET, get comfortable, and let's go!

1. First, turn on the PET. This is done with a rocker switch at the left rear of the cabinet. After a few moments you will see a message starting with **COMMO-DORE BASIC** and ending with READY. READY, and the flashing square of light (called the "cursor"), indicates that PET is ready for business. Now type

?1+4

and stop. Has anything happened?

_____

Now press RETURN and record below what PET did.

_____

2. Now you know how to make PET do addition. Let's explore this some more. Type

$$?20.1+54$$

and press RETURN. What happened?

_____

3. Type

$$?2+4-3$$

and press RETURN. Record the output below.

_____

4. All right, the + and – are simple enough. Type the following expression

$$?12/2$$

and press RETURN. What happened?

_____

What arithmetic operation does the / call for?

_____

5. If, when typing in material, you make an error, it can be deleted with the DEL key at the upper right corner of the keyboard. Each time the DEL key is pressed, one character will disappear from the screen, moving from right to left. When you press the RETURN key, PET may come back with SYNTAX ERROR. If this happens, try to see what the problem is and retype the line.

6. Your PET screen should be fairly full now. Press the CLR key. Remember that you will have to hold the SHIFT key down while pressing the key with CLR on it. What happened?

_____

7. Now that you know how, you can clear the screen any time you desire. If the screen is full and new lines are entered, lines will scroll off the top. Let's go on exploring the calculator mode. Type

?2*50

and press RETURN. What happened?

_____

What arithmetic operation is called for by the *?

_____

8. Type in the following expression but don't press RETURN when finished.

?(2+3)*4-1

What will happen when you press RETURN?

_____

Press RETURN and record below what did happen.

_____

9. Now on to a new wrinkle. Type

PRINT 2+3*(4-1)

and press RETURN. What did PET do?

_____

10. Type

PRINT "2+3*(4-1)"

and press RETURN. Record below what happened.

_____

11. What will happen if you type

PRINT "BAD DOG"

and press RETURN?

_____

Try it and see if you were correct.

12. Now let's move on to a different topic. First, clear the screen. If you have forgotten how, look back at step 6. Find the two blue keys labeled CRSR at the upper right of the keyboard. These keys are used to move the cursor over the screen. Experiment with these keys until you can move the cursor to any point on the screen you desire. Specifically, move the cursor down to the lower right corner of the screen. Press HOME. What happened?

_____

Of course, the HOME key moves the cursor to the home position from any point on the screen. You should try this by moving the cursor to various places on the screen and then pressing the HOME key.

13. Now type in the characters shown below.

A B C D E
1 2 3 4 5

Don't press the RETURN key while doing this. Move the cursor around with the CRSR keys as needed.

14. Now place the cursor over the letter A and type the letter F. What happened?

_____

15. Change the 3 to an 8, the C to an X, and the 5 to a 9. Then change the pattern back to the original one shown in step 13.

16. Now clear the screen and create the word PET in large block letters using the graphic character that is the upper function on the "&" key. Move the cursor around as needed with the CRSR keys. Don't press the RETURN key while doing this. To help you get started, move the cursor down a few lines and out to the right a few spaces. Now press the upper "&" key five times, the space key, five more upper "&" characters, the space key, and finally five more upper "&" characters. This should appear as on the screen as follows:

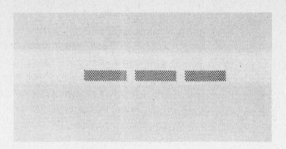

The three bars on the screen form the tops of the letters P, E, and T. Now by building on these bars, the letters can be completed as shown below.

Again, don't press the RETURN key while completing the block letters. Move the cursor around as needed with the cursor controls.

17. If desired, you can create intricate graphic designs using the graphic characters in the upper position on the keys. Later on we will learn how to write programs to create pictures. For now, simply see how the graphic characters appear on the screen.

18. Turn off the PET and go on to the discussion material.

2-3 DISCUSSION

Now we will go back over the topics that you have just worked with on the PET. With this experience you will be in a far better position to understand the discussion.

Turning PET On and Off

The PET has to be one of the easiest computers ever built to turn ON and OFF! As you have already seen, this is done with a simple rocker switch at the left rear of the cabinet. When PET is turned on, you are greeted with a message like:

```
**COMMODORE BASIC**
 7167 BYTES FREE
READY
```

Because the amount of memory in various PETs differs, you may see a number other than 7167 in the welcoming message. The term "byte" is used to describe a single character of storage. Thus "7167 BYTES FREE" means that there are 7167 characters of storage free in which you can work.

One last point; if at any time things get away from you, if you have lost touch, or if PET seems out of control, you have a foolproof escape mechanism. Simply turn your PET off and then back on. All the former ills will be forgotten and PET will once again be ready for business. This remedy is not without disadvantage, however, since you will lose any programs or information in memory at the time you turned PET off. However, it is an absolute way for you to regain control.

Calculator Mode

In the discovery activities you learned how to do simple arithmetic operations using PET like a simple calculator. This is also known as the "immediate execution" mode. As we shall see in the next chapter, BASIC stores instructions and commands in a series of numbered lines, and then is directed by you to perform all the instructions at the same time. If, however, the instructions are typed in without a line number, PET assumes you want an immediate answer and does what you asked it to do, if possible.

Recall that when you were using PET in the immediate execution mode, you typed in a question mark before the arithmetic instructions. You can think of the question mark as a "what is" question. Thus,

$$?5*3.2+6.3$$

asks PET "what is 5 times 3.2 added to 6.3?" When you press RETURN, PET obliges with the answer 22.3.

Also, you should have noticed that putting PRINT before arithmetic commands causes the same thing to happen as when the question mark is used. Therefore

$$PRINT\ 5*3.2+6.3$$

asks PET to once again compute what 5 times 3.2 plus 6.3 is, and to print out the result. Internally PET treats "?" and "PRINT" exactly the same. How you chose to think about the commands (either "what is so and so," or "compute so and so, and print out the results") is a matter of individual preference.

When material is typed in, PET doesn't do anything until you press RETURN. The RETURN key tells PET you are through typing. When you are through typing anything at all and want to let PET know, press the RETURN key.

We have discovered that addition and subtraction are called for by + and –, which probably wasn't much of a surprise! Multiplication and division are indicated by * and / respectively. Parentheses can be used to group operations any way desired. There are a number of other clever operations that can be done, but we will postpone discussion of these to later chapters.

Finally, if you type

```
?"ABCDEFG"
```

or

```
PRINT "ABCDEFG"
```

and press RETURN, PET is instructed to print out the collection of characters between the quotation marks – in this case, the letters ABCDEFG. Such a collection is called a "character string," and is an important concept which we will return to throughout the balance of the book.

Screen Editing

Editing or changes in the screen display are done with the cursor (the flashing square of light). As you type in characters, the cursor indicates where the next character will be placed on the screen. The CRSR keys allow you to move the cursor around the screen as desired.

When the CRSR keys are used, the cursor moves over the characters on the screen without changing them. However, if the cursor is over a character and you press a key, that character will replace the one under the cursor on the screen.

Characters can be deleted using the DEL key. This causes the character to the left of the cursor to be deleted. All characters to the right of the cursor will shifted over one position. There are additional tricky ways of doing screen editing, but the few simple tools explained above will suffice for now.

Screen Graphics

The full capability of PET graphics requires contol by a BASIC program. As we go through the balance of the book, examples and problems will be included which will gradually build up your graphic skills.

Right now, however, you must be content with a careful inspection of the graphic characters that can be used. With several exceptions, each of the keys on the PET keyboard has an upper function that is a graphic character. Careful examination of the symbols and shapes involved with these characters reveals an almost unlimited set of graphic displays that can be drawn. Probably the best thing for you do do at this point is to experiment with various combinations of graphic characters to see what can be done. Later on we will see how to become more proficient and generate screen graphics under BASIC program control.

2-4 PRACTICE TEST

Take the test below to discover how well you have learned the objectives of Chapter 2. The answers to the practice test are given at the end of the book.

1. When you are through typing a line, how do you let PET know?

_____

2. If you lose control of PET, how can you regain it?

_____

3. What symbol is used to indicate multiplication on PET?

_____

4. How do you clear the screen on PET?

_____

5. What operation does the symbol / indicate to PET?

_____

6. What will happen if you type

?3*4/6

and then press RETURN?

_____

7. What will happen if you type

PRINT "25+12/4"

and then press RETURN?

_____

8. Suppose you have typed in some material, then use the CRSR keys to move the cursor back into the line just typed.If you press the DEL key twice, describe exactly what will happen.

_____

THREE

INTRODUCTION TO BASIC

Now we are ready to begin learning about BASIC. In this chapter we will see how to write and execute some very simple programs.

3-1 OBJECTIVES

The objectives are simple but important as they are your first introduction to BASIC. The objectives are listed below.

Requirements for BASIC Programs

All BASIC programs have common characteristics. We will look at some very simple programs to learn about these characteristics.

Telling PET What to Do

System commands are used to tell PET to do something to or with a BASIC program. These action words are used to control a program. We will look at the following system commands: LIST, RUN, STOP, and NEW.

Entering and Controlling Programs

This objective overlaps the one above. The main thing we want to accomplish is to make you comfortable when entering and controlling programs. All the programs we will encounter initially are short and easy to handle.

Variable Names in BASIC

Since only certain combinations of characters may be used to name (or stand for) numbers or character strings in BASIC, we must know these well.

3-2 DISCOVERY ACTIVITIES

In the computer work that follows you will be directed to enter various programs. If you see a <CR> in the instructions, press the RETURN key. Remember from your experiences in Chapter 2 that pressing the RETURN key tells PET you are through typing. Now go on to the activities on the next page.

1. Turn on your PET, and after the welcoming message ending with READY is displayed, type in

$$100 \quad A = 1 \quad <CR>$$

This is the first line of a BASIC program.

2. Now type in the balance of the program as listed below.

```
110 B = 8    <CR>
120 C = A+B    <CR>
130 PRINT C    <CR>
140 END    <CR>
```

If you make mistakes while typing in the program, correct the errors using the cursor and the methods learned in Chapter 2.

3. Press the CLR key (remember to hold down the SHIFT key while doing this) and clear the screen. What happened to the program you just typed in?

_____

4. Fortunately, all is not lost. PET has remembered what you typed in even though the screen is blank. Type LIST and press the RETURN key. What happened?

_____

5. At the top of the screen you should see the program just entered. For the time being, ignore the line numbers at the beginning of each line. Just read the lines in the program and try to get a sense of what they mean. If PET is told to carry out the instructions, what do you think will happen?

_____

Type RUN and press the RETURN key. What did happen?

_____

6. All right, run the cursor up to line 110 and place it over the 8. Press the 5 key and then the RETURN key. Clear the screen with the CLR key, type LIST, and then press the RETURN key. What has happened to line 110 in the program?

_____

7. If you tell PET to execute this program what do you think will happen?

_____

Type RUN and press the RETURN key. Were you right?

_____

8. Now type

140   <CR>

Clear the screen and display the program using the LIST command. What has happened to line 140?

_____

If you want to delete a line in a BASIC program, how do you do it?

_____

9. Now RUN the program. What happened?

_____

Does the END statement that formerly was in statement 140 appear to be required by PET?

_____

10. Let's experiment a bit more. Often we want to clear out the program in PET's memory. This is done with the NEW command. Type NEW and press the RETURN key. Did anything appear to happen?

_____

Clear the screen and LIST the program to see what PET has in memory. Is anything there?

_____

11. We have learned how to clear out a program in memory, but now have no program left! To get our program back we must enter it again. Type in the program below.

```
100 A = 1     <CR>
110 B = 8     <CR>
120 C = A+B   <CR>
130 PRINT C   <CR>
140 END    <CR>
```

Check all the lines to make sure they were entered correctly. If a line needs to be changed, move the cursor over the error, correct it, and press the RETURN key. Finally, clear the screen and redisplay the program by typing LIST.

12. Now type

```
125 D = B-A   <CR>
135 PRINT D   <CR>
```

Clear the screen and display the program. What has happened?

_____

13. Take a few minutes to study the program. What will happen if you RUN the program?

_____

Type RUN, press the RETURN key, and record below what PET did.

_____

14. In the original program the line numbers were not consecutive (like 100, 101, 102, 103, etc.) but had gaps (e.g., 100, 110, 120, 130, and 140). Can you think of a reason for doing this now? (Hint: See step 12.)

_____

15. How do you insert lines in a BASIC program? (Hint: See steps 12 and 14.)

_____

16. Clear out the program in PET'S memory by typing NEW and pressing the RETURN key. Clear the screen and enter the program below.

```
100 INPUT A    <CR>
110 B = A+2    <CR>
120 PRINT B    <CR>
130 GOTO 100    <CR>
140 END    <CR>
```

17. This new program has several features that you have not seen before. Study the program carefully and think about what will happen if we RUN the program. What does the GOTO 100 in line 130 mean?

_____

18. Now RUN the program and record what PET did.

_____

Type the numeral 6 and press the RETURN key. What happened?

_____

19. Type the numeral 10 and press the RETURN key. What took place?

_____

20. What line in the program do you think is generating the question mark?

_____

Describe in your own words what the program is doing. If necessary, experiment some more to make sure you are correct.

_____

21. Now we want to get out of the program. Press the RETURN key. What happened?

_____

22. Clear out the program in PET's memory. Type in the following program.

```
100 A = 1    <CR>
110 PRINT A    <CR>
120 A = A+1    <CR>
130 GOTO 110    <CR>
140 END    <CR>
```

23. RUN the program and record below what happened.

_____

When you get tired watching the display, press the STOP key. What happened?

_____

24. Try it once more. RUN the program and after a few numbers are typed out, interrupt the program. How do you stop a BASIC program running on PET?

_____

25. Clear the screen and display the program in memory. Type the lines below. Note the absences of spaces in the first line and the extra spaces in the second.

```
100A=1    <CR>
1 2 0 A = A + 1    <CR>
```

Now clear the screen and LIST the program. See what happened to the spacing in the lines above. We Will return to this matter later.

26. Let's try a program with some new features. Clear the program from memory by typing NEW and then pressing the RETURN key. Clear the screen and type in the program below.

```
100 PRINT "TYPE IN A NUMBER"    <CR>
110 INPUT A    <CR>
120 PRINT "TYPE IN ANOTHER NUMBER"    <CR>
130 INPUT B    <CR>
140 C = A+B    <CR>
150 PRINT "THEIR SUM IS"    <CR>
160 PRINT C    <CR>
170 END    <CR>
```

27. Study the program for a few moments. Now RUN the program. What happened?

_____

Type the numeral 12, press the RETURN key, and record below what PET did.

_____

28. All right, now type the numeral 13, press the RETURN key, and record below what happened.

_____

This simple program illustrates that we can arrange for BASIC programs to print out messages as well as numbers.

29. Clear out the program in memory and clear the screen. In the program below the blanks after the quotation marks in each line are put there using the SPACE key. You can find the special graphic characters in the upper, or shift, position on the keyboard. Now enter the program below remembering to press the RETURN key at the end of each line.

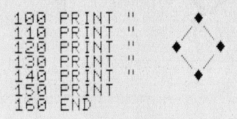

```
100 PRINT "        ◆
110 PRINT "       ⟋ ⟍
120 PRINT "      ◆   ◆
130 PRINT "       ⟍ ⟋
140 PRINT "        ◆
150 PRINT
160 END
```

30. As you can probably guess, this program will produce a graphic design on the screen. Clear the screen and RUN the program to verify that the pattern is produced as predicted.

31. Now if we make a small change in the program, we can make dramatic changes in the results. Type in the following program line.

155 GOTO 100   <CR>

RUN the program and watch the display. While the display is flashing by, hold down the RVS key and observe the effect. If you release the RVS key, the display will speed up again. Press the STOP key to halt the program.

32. Clear out the program in PET's memory, clear the screen, and enter the program below.

```
100 PRINT "DOG   ";    <CR>
110 GOTO 100    <CR>
120 END
```

Note the three spaces after DOG in line 100. Clear the screen and RUN the program. After watching the display for a while, press the STOP key to halt the program.

33. Now let's look at a different topic. Press the CLR key to clear the screen. Type NEW and press the RETURN key to clear the program from memory. Then enter the following program:

```
100 A = 1    <CR>
110 A$ = "HOUSE"    <CR>
120 PRINT A    <CR>
130 PRINT "A"    <CR>
140 PRINT A$    <CR>
150 PRINT "A$"    <CR>
160 END    <CR>
```

34. This program contains something new. Look at the A$ in line 110. Note that it is set equal to a word enclosed in quotation marks. The balance of the program has to do with variations on printing out A and A$. RUN the program and record the output.

---

35. Study the output carefully and identify what PET printed in response to each of

the PRINT statements. For the time being just make the comparison. Later we will examine the subject in detail. Enter the following line:

```
155 PRINT B    <CR>
```

36. Clear the screen and display the program with the LIST command. Note that the only place B is mentioned is in line 155 in the PRINT statement. What do you think will happen if we RUN the program?

_____

OK, now RUN the program and record what happened.

_____

As you saw, even though the value of B was not defined in the program, PET assigned it a value of 0. This is an important fact to be considered while writing programs. We will return to the issue later.

37. This concludes the discovery work for this chapter. Turn your PET off and go on to the next section.

Look: either speak our language or back to the supermarket!

710 LET B = 3
720 ‖ ‖‖‖ ‖ ‖ ■ ‖ ‖

3-3 DISCUSSION

Now that you have been through the computer work at your PET and have seen some of the features of BASIC in action, we can summarize what has taken place.

Correcting Mistakes

Since most of us make mistakes while typing, we need to be able to correct errors sent to PET. Suppose a mistake is made while you are typing a line. How it is corrected depends upon whether you have pressed the RETURN key yet, and where the error is. If you press the RETURN key, the line you have been typing (mistake included) is analyzed by PET. Some errors will be picked up at this point in which case PET may type out SYNTAX ERROR indicating some problem it cannot handle.

If you have not pressed the RETURN key, and notice the mistake, you have two options open. First, you can move the cursor to the mistake, correct it, move the cursor to the end of the material that has already been entered, and then finish the line. Or, you can press the DEL key as many times as necessary to delete characters back to the mistake, then type the balance of the line correctly.

Sometimes you may need to insert characters in a line. This can be done with the INST key. If you press this key, all the characters in the line at the position of the cursor and to the right are shifted to the right one place. This opens up a blank space for your use.

Some errors may not show up until you RUN the program. If PET detects an error at this point, it will type out an error message and an associated line number. Suppose PET found an error in line 350. You could type LIST 350–350 to cause the line in question to be printed on the screen. Now you can use the screen editing capability to correct the error. Remember that following the correction, you must press the RETURN key to make the correction in memory.

Requirements for BASIC Programs

Several important facts about BASIC programs have been demonstrated. To have a program to use for discussion purposes, we will return to the original program used in the computer work:

```
100 A = 1
110 B = 8
120 C = A+B
130 PRINT C
140 END
```

Each BASIC program consists of a group of lines called "statements." Each statement must have a line number. In the program above, there are three types of BASIC statements: assignment (identified by the = sign), PRINT, and END. The first two will be treated fully in the next chapter. For the time being, the use of each of these statements in the program is clear. The END statement, however, has particular significance. The last statement in a program should be the END statement. As you saw in the computer work, PET doesn't require that the END statement be present. However, it is probably a good plan to use the END statement in your programs. The END statement is a clear marker that the program is finished. If the END statement is not used, a reader might wonder if the program were complete or not. If the END statement is used, it must have the highest line number in the program.

Generally the line numbers in a BASIC program are not numbered consecutively (such as 100, 101, 102, etc.). The reason is that we may want to insert additional statements later if we discover errors or want to modify the program. If the lines were numbered consecutively, changes would involve retyping the entire program. With gaps in the line numbers, statements can be inserted by simply typing in the new statements using line numbers not already in the program.

PET does not care what order the lines in a BASIC program are entered. If, for example, we type

```
140 END
120 C = A+B
110 B = 8
130 PRINT C
100 A = 1
```

and this new program is displayed, PET will sort out the statements and display them in numerical order. In the same way, if we told PET to RUN the program, the statements would be sorted into numerical order before starting execution.

You can remove a BASIC statement from a program by typing the line number and pressing the RETURN key. Statements can be modified by retyping the lines involved, pressing the RETURN key after each line is typed. As indicated above, statements can be added by using line numbers not already in the program. Thus, BASIC statements can be added, removed, or changed as desired. The ability to change programs easily is one of the powerful characteristics of BASIC. The screen editing capability makes the PET version of BASIC even more flexible.

One last point about BASIC involves spaces in the statements. In the computer work you were directed to type in two lines, one with no spaces, the other with extra spaces inserted. As you saw, PET made some changes in the spaces when the program was displayed with the LIST command. Generally, PET will insert a space between the line number and the rest of the line. Spaces in the balance of the line are left as is. To be on the safe side, type in the statements as you want them to appear.

Telling PET What to Do

We must make a sharp distinction between the statements in a BASIC program and system commands. System commands tell PET to do something with a program. We have seen several of these in the computer work and will briefly review the use of each.

Quite often we want PET to type out the program it has in memory. This could be because of changes in the program that produce a cluttered screen. Or, you and PET may be in a state of mutual confusion about the program. The way to resolve the issue is to instruct PET to display the program in its memory. This is done with the LIST command. If you type LIST and then press the RETURN key, PET will display the program on the screen. Usually, you would clear the screen first so a clean copy of the program would be displayed. If the program has more than 25 lines and is displayed with the LIST command, only the final 25 lines will be displayed. Everything before the final 25 lines will scroll off the top of the screen. By modifying the LIST command though, we can look at any part of a program we desire no matter how big the program. If, for example, we type LIST 300-400, PET will display those BASIC statements in the program from 300 to 400 inclusive. Or, LIST -200 will cause PET to print out all the program statements from the beginning of the program up to line 200. Finally, LIST 400- will instruct PET to display the program lines from 400 through the end of the program. Clearly, you can change the numbers involved in the LIST command to look at any part of the program you desire.

A BASIC program is simply a set of instructions to be acted upon by the computer. However, PET needs to be told to start this process. This is done with the RUN command. When the RUN command is received, PET goes to the lowest numbered statement in the program, carries out the instructions, goes to the next higher numbered statement, and keeps on carrying out instructions in numerical order, unless the program directs a statement to be done out of order. Remember then, when you want PET to start acting on the instructions contained in a BASIC program, type RUN and press the RETURN key.

Suppose you are finished working with a program and decide to go on to another. You can clear the screen, but this does not clear the current program out of memory. PET has one portion of memory that keeps track of what is to be displayed on the screen. A separate part of memory holds the current program. Thus, the CLR key signals PET to clear out everything in the screen portion of memory. The NEW command is used to erase the current program in memory. You saw in the computer work that the NEW command has no effect upon the screen display. Since, as we now know, two different parts of memory are involved, this should cause no confusion. You should be careful to use the NEW command when you are finished with a program. If the old program is not erased, a new program goes into the same space with the very confusing result that PET may have parts of two different programs in memory.

Entering and Controlling Programs

So far, when you have been instructed to type in commands or program statements, the <CR> prompt was given to remind you to press the RETURN key. This habit should be well developed by now, so we will not use the <CR> prompt in further work.

Situations come up where we need to be able to control a program that is running. Certainly one of the most dramatic cases is when a program is in a closed loop and will keep on running forever if we don't interrupt it. We can break into such a program by pressing the STOP key. When this is done, PET breaks the program execution, tells us what line was being executed when the interruption took place, and types READY indicating it is once more ready to receive commands. A different problem is when PET is in an input loop waiting for a number to be typed in. If we want to get out of such a situation, press the RETURN key instead of entering the number. PET then jumps out of the program execution back to the READY mode.

One final feature of the PET needs to be discussed in this section involving entering and controlling programs. When a program is being displayed with the LIST command, or when numerical output is being printed on the screen, the rate at which the display is being presented can be slowed down by holding down the RVS key. Actually, RVS stands for "reverse field" and is normally used to cause PET to reverse the light and dark areas in the characters as they are displayed. We will discuss this feature later. For the time being, though, you should be aware of the dual function of this particular key. The function we are concerned with here is the ability to slow down the rate at which display is generated on the screen.

Variable Names in BASIC

Now we come to one of the ideas in BASIC that most often causes problems for the beginner. It concerns variable names and the distinction between the name and the quantity stored in memory under that name. In the BASIC statement

$$100 \ A \ = \ 2$$

the letter A names a variable. By "variable" we mean that different values can be assigned to A. Statements that have an = sign in them are called "assignment" statements. In the case above, the variable A is assigned the value 2. Actually, what is taking place is that PET has named a memory location A, and has stored a 2 in that location. You must be careful to separate the name of a location in memory from the contents of that location. It's the same notion as the difference between a post office box number and the contents of that box. The box number does not change, but the contents of the box may be changed at any time.

Another issue should be mentioned with regard to the assignment statement. Some versions of BASIC use a LET in the assignment statement. An example might be

$$100 \ LET \ A \ = \ 2$$

Usually, the use of the LET in assignment statements is optional. This is the case as far as PET is concerned. Since the use of the LET in the assignment statements contributes nothing to the programs, we will not use LET in this book. The only reason for raising the issue is that if you read other books, you will more than likely see the LET employed in the assignment statements.

Consider the following statement.

$$130 \ C \ = \ A+B$$

This instructs PET to get the numbers stored in locations named A and B, add them together, and put the sum in the storage location named C. The equal sign means to evaluate what is on the right and assign it to the variable named on the left.

To pursue this issue further, suppose we have a BASIC statement such as

$$120 \ B \ = \ B+1$$

If we consider the statement above as an algebraic equation, we have

$$B = B + 1$$

By subtracting B from both sides of this equation we have

$$0 = 1$$

which is very strange indeed! It is certainly clear that the = sign in a BASIC statement does not mean the same as it does in an algebraic equation. Instead, the statement

$$120 \ B \ = \ B+1$$

instructs the computer to get the number stored in location B, add 1 to the number, and put the result back into the storage location named B.

If we store a number in a location, anything that was stored there before is lost. Consider the following statements:

$$100 \ A \ = \ 1$$
$$110 \ A \ = \ 2*3$$

Line 100 instructs the computer to set up a storage location called A and put the number 1 in that location. Line 120 tells PET to multiply 2 by 3 and store the product in memory location A. Note that the 1 stored previously in memory location A has been lost.

This brings us to the heart of the issue. The letter A, which identifies a storage location, is called a variable because the contents of A can be changed. The name of the location does not change, but the number stored there can be changed as desired.

To be precise, the variable A referred to above is called a "numeric" variable. The reason for including "numeric" in the name is that there is another type of variable called a "character-string." You were introduced to this concept briefly in the computer work, and now we must tie up some loose ends.

As far as names are concerned, it is easy to distinguish between numeric and character-string variables. A, B, M, and P would all identify numeric variables and name numeric quantities. A$, B$, M$, and P$ all name strings of characters. The $ symbol that is appended identifies the name as a character-string variable. In the BASIC statement

$$100 \ B\$ \ = \ "BARN"$$

B$ names a location in memory at which the character-string "BARN" is stored. The quotation marks set off the string, but are not part of it.

In BASIC, only certain names can be used for variables whether they are numeric or character-string. PET has quite relaxed rules for these names compared with most computers. With regard to numeric variables, a letter (A through Z), or a letter and a single digit (A0, A1, and so on to Z8, Z9), or two letters (AA, AB, AC and so on to ZY, ZZ) can be used for names. If you append a $ sign, the result is a name for a character string variable. Thus, A$, C8$, and XY$ are acceptable names for character-strings.

You can add additional characters to the names, but PET pays attention only to the first two and checks for the presence of the $ sign. This is an easy way to get into trouble. Consider the following BASIC statements:

```
100 HEAT$ = "HORSE
110 HEAR$ = "COW"
120 PRINT HEAR$, HEAT$
130 END
```

If we were to RUN this program, PET would print out COW COW. The reason is that HEAT$ and HEAR$ are the same names for character-strings as far as PET is concerned, since it checks only the first two letters and the $ sign. The statement in line 110 undoes what was accomplished in line 100.

Let's go over the important points once more. A variable name in BASIC identifies a storage location in memory. If the variable is numeric, a number is stored in the memory location. If the variable is a character-string, a collection of characters is stored in the memory location. The contents of the storage location can be modified, but the names of the storage locations remain the same.

The assignment statement evaluates what is on the right side of the equal sign and assigns it to the storage location named on the left side. Thus,

$$100 \quad D = A+B+C$$

instructs the computer to evaluate the expression (A+B+C) using the numbers stored in memory locations named A, B, and C. The results are then stored in the memory location named D.

We have just scratched the surface with regard to character–string variables. We will return to this topic several times during the balance of the book.

3-4 PRACTICE TEST

Take the test below to discover how well you have learned the objectives of Chapter 3. The answers to the practice test are given at the end of the book.

1. How do you signal PET you are through typing a line or a command?

_____

2. Suppose that PET is waiting at an INPUT statement in a program for you to enter a number. You decide instead that you want to jump out of the program. How do you do this?

_____

3. How do you interrupt a program that is running on your computer?

_____

4. What is wrong with the following program?

```
100 A = 1
110 B = 3
120 C = B-A
PRINT C
130 END
```

_____

5. Why should an END statement be used in BASIC programs even though PET doesn't require it?

_____

6. How do you remove a line from a BASIC program?

_____

7. How do you insert a line in a BASIC program?

_____

8. How do you replace a line in a BASIC program?

_____

9. How do you display the program in memory?

_____

2041014

10. How do you erase the screen?

_____

11. How do you erase a program from memory?

_____

12. How do you command PET to start executing a program in memory?

_____

13. What are the permissible names for numeric variables in BASIC?

_____

14. What are the permissible names for character-string variables in BASIC?

_____

FOUR

COMPUTER ARITHMETIC AND PROGRAM MANAGEMENT

4-1 OBJECTIVES

Now that you have been introduced to BASIC on the PET, we are ready to go on to more interesting tasks.

Arithmetic on the Computer

Ultimately, all mathematics on a computer is done using the simplest arithmetic operations. It is essential to have a clear understanding of how these arithmetic operations are done.

Parentheses ( ) in Computations

As we shall see, all mathematical expressions must be typed on a single line to enter them into the PET. Some expressions can be handled this way only by organizing parts of the expression in parentheses. Thus, the effective use of parentheses is a necessary skill.

E Notation for Numbers

PET must deal with both very large and very small numbers. "E notation" is used by PET to describe such numbers. We need to be able to recognize and interpret E notation since PET may type out numbers in this form.

Storing and Retrieving Programs

We have already seen some system commands. Additional system commands will be introduced in this chapter, which will permit us to store and retrieve programs from the magnetic tape unit that is an integral part of PET.

4-2 DISCOVERY ACTIVITIES

The discovery activities in this chapter introduce the characteristics of computer arithmetic on the PET. Additional system commands for program management will be explored.

Now let's go on to the computer work for this chapter.

1. Turn your PET on and type in the following program:

```
100 INPUT A
110 INPUT B
120 C = A+B
130 PRINT C
140 END
```

What arithmetic operation is called for by the + in line 120?

_____

2. Let's see if you are right. RUN the program. When PET goes to line 100, it will type out a question mark, halt, and wait for you to type in a value for A. In this case,

type in 10. The computer will then go to line 110, type out a question mark, halt, and wait for you to type in a value for B. Type in 20. What did the computer print out?

_____

3. Using the cursor, change the + in line 120 to –, and then press RETURN. Clear the screen and LIST the program. RUN the program and at the first question mark (INPUT prompt) type in 30 for A and at the second prompt, type in 12 for B. What happened?

_____

What arithmetic operation is done with the – in line 120?

_____

4. Change the – in line 120 to * using the cursor as described above. Clear the screen and display the program. RUN the program and type in 5 for A, and 6 for B when the INPUT prompts (question marks) come up. What did PET type out?

_____

What arithmetic operation does the * call for?

_____

5. Now change the * in line 120 to /. RUN the program and when the INPUT prompts come up, enter 45 for A and 15 for B. What did PET type out?

_____

What arithmetic operation does the / call for?

_____

6. Thus far we have seen only a single arithmetic operation on a line. Let's look at an example in which there is more than one operation. Type

$$120 \quad C = A+B-B/3$$

Clear the screen, display the program and study it briefly. If we RUN the program now and enter 2 for A and 3 for B, what do you think will happen?

_____

RUN the program, enter the values above, and write down what happened.

_____

7. Clear out the program in PET's memory by typing NEW and pressing the RETURN key. Then clear the screen and type

```
100 A = 3*3
110 B = 3↑2
120 PRINT A
130 PRINT B
140 END
```

Make sure you have entered the program correctly. Then RUN the program and record the results below.

_____

Compare the numbers printed out with the expressions in the lines where they were computed. See if you can figure out what is taking place.

8. Change lines 100 and 110 to read as follows:

```
100 A = 3*3*3
110 B = 3↑3
```

RUN the program and write down what PET did.

_____

9. Change lines 100 and 110 to read as follows:

```
100 A = 2*2*2*2
110 B = 2↑4
```

RUN the program. What happened?

_____

What is the ↑ symbol used for in BASIC?

_____

10. Clear the screen and the program in memory. Enter the following program:

```
100 A = 4+2*6/3
110 B = (4+2)*6/3
120 C = 4+(2*6)/3
130 D = 4+2*(6/3)
140 PRINT A
150 PRINT B
160 PRINT C
170 PRINT D
180 END
```

The two points of this program are (1) the order in which the arithmetic is done, and (2) the effect of the parentheses. If you look closely, it is clear that the same numbers are involved in each of the calculations in lines 100, 110, 120, and 130. The only difference is the grouping in the lines. RUN the program and record what PET did.

_____

Study the program and the numbers PET typed out until you see what is taking place in the program. There are very specific rules that PET uses in such situations. If you aren't able to see clearly what these rules are, don't worry; we will go over the topic completely later in the chapter.

11. Clear the screen with the CLR key. Clear the program in memory with the NEW command. Now enter the following program:

```
100 A = 3*100
110 B = 3*100*100*100
120 C = 3*100*100*100*100*100
130 PRINT A
140 PRINT B
150 PRINT C
160 END
```

RUN the program and record the output.

_____

Can you explain the different forms in which the numbers were typed out? (Hint: Count the numbers of zeros in the multipliers in lines 100, 110, and 120 in the program.)

12. Change the first three lines in the program to read as follows:

```
100 A = 3/100
110 B = 3/(100*100*100)
120 C = 3/(100*100*100*100*100)
```

RUN the program and record the output.

_____

Again, can you see what is taking place in the output? Count the zeros in the denominators in lines 100, 110, and 120.

13. If an E shows up in a number typed out by PET, what does it mean? Explain in your own words.

_____

If you still do not fully understand the purpose of the E notation, relax! We will return to it later.

14. Obtain a clear tape cassette and place it in the tape unit on PET. Press the REW key to rewind the tape. When the unit stops turning, press the STOP key on the tape unit. Clear the screen and redisplay the program we have been working with in step 13. Now type the following:

SAVE "EXAMPLE"

What happened?

_____

Now follow the instructions by pressing the REC and PLAY keys on the tape unit at the same time. What did PET do?

_____

15. When the program has been recorded, PET will write READY on the screen. When you see this, press the STOP key on the tape unit. Now clear the screen and use the NEW command to remove the program from memory. Enter the following program:

```
100 A = 1000
110 PRINT A
120 END
```

16. Now type

```
SAVE "SAMPLE"
```

and record below what happened.

_____

Press REC and PLAY on the tape unit at the same time and write down what happened.

_____

17. Rewind the tape by pressing the REW key, and when complete press the STOP key on the tape unit. Now type

```
LOAD "SAMPLE"
```

and record what PET did.

_____

All right, press PLAY on the tape unit. What happened? (It will take a few moments.)

_____

18. LIST the program to verify that "SAMPLE" has been loaded from the tape unit. Press REW to rewind the tape, then press the STOP key on the tape unit. Now type

```
LOAD "EXAMPLE"
```

and follow the instructions printed out by PET. Once the program has been loaded, you should display it to verify that you have the right one.

19. This completes the computer work for now. Remove your tape cassette, turn the PET off, and go on to the next section.

4-3 DISCUSSION

A number of very important points have been introduced in the computer work. Probably you didn't meet with too much difficulty going through the discovery material, but this shouldn't make you ignore the fundamental ideas involved. Lack of understanding at this point will return to haunt you later on in the book. Consequently we will go over each of the objectives of the chapter in great detail to ensure that they are mastered.

Arithmetic on the Computer

We are concerned with five arithmetic operations. These are addition, subtraction, multiplication, division, and exponentiation. The first four are certainly familiar to you, and the last (exponentiation) might be frightening mainly because of the fierce-looking word used to define the process. Let's go over each of these operations and see how PET handles them.

Addition and subtraction are done precisely as you would expect. The symbols used to define the operations (+ and -) mean the same thing to PET that they mean in mathematics classes.

Multiplication is handled the same way on the computer as in arithmetic but has a different symbol to define the process, the * character. Thus 2*3 is 6. A*B signals PET to look up the numbers stored in A and B, then multiply them together.

Division is indicated with the / symbol. A/B means to divide the number stored in location A by the one stored in B. Likewise, 8/2 means to divide 8 by 2.

Finally, the exponentiation operation is defined by the ↑ symbol. Exponentiation means "raised to the power." Therefore, 3↑4 means "3 raised to the fourth power," which in turn means 3 multiplied by itself four times, giving 81 as the result.

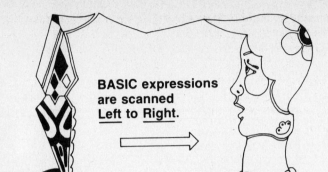

BASIC expressions are scanned Left to Right.

We must be very careful to understand the order in which arithmetic operations are done by PET. Consider the following expression:

$$2+3\uparrow2/5-1$$

If the computer simply goes through the expression from the left, performing operations as they are met, the result would be 2 plus 3 (giving 5), raised to the second power (giving 25), divided by 5 (giving 5), minus 1, producing an answer of 4. However, suppose addition and subtraction are done first, then exponentiation, then multiplication and division. This would give 5 raised to the second power (giving 25), divided by 4, for an answer of 6.25.

Priority rules are:
1st—   ^ or ↑
2d—   * and
3d—   + and

Clearly, we could go on with different rules for the order of arithmetic operations and might get different answers each time. The point is that there are well-defined rules in BASIC for the order and priority of arithmetic operations, and we must understand them. Here they are:

The order of operations is from left to right using the priority rules given below.

The priority for arithmetic operations is (1) exponentiation, (2) multiplication and division, and (3) addition and subtraction.

Now, if we go back to our example of

$$2+3\uparrow2/5-1$$

we scan left to right for any exponentiation. Since there is an exponentiation indicated (3↑2), it is done first. Now the expression is

$$2+9/5-1$$

Scanning from left to right, we again look for exponentiation, and finding none, look for operations with the next highest priority (multiplication and division). The division is therefore done next, with the following result:

$$2+1.8-1$$

Since there are no more multiplications or divisions left in the expression, we scan from left to right for addition and subtraction. The addition gives

$$3.8-1$$

and the final subtraction produces the answer of 2.8.

Review the rules for order and priority until they become second nature to you. We will look at the rules again when the use of parentheses is discussed in the next section.

Parentheses in Computations

The rules for order and priority of arithmetic are not the whole issue, however. There is often a bit more involved. To see this, consider the following more complicated example:

```
        ┌──────────── B────┐
      ┌──────── A─┐     ┌─ C ─┐
      ((2*3+4↑2)*2+5)*(3↑2−4)
```

Obviously, the difference between this expression and the ones we have been studying is the use of parentheses to group parts of the expression. We will go through this example in great detail to show you how PET attacks the arithmetic involved.

PET starts by scanning from left to right and meets the left parenthesis of B. It then looks inside to see if there are any left parentheses and finds one for A. The next parenthesis met is a right parenthesis for A. At this point, PET has isolated the first group of operations to be done. This is

$$2*3+4↑2$$

and is evaluated using the order and priority rules. The result is 22 (check it). Now our problem has become

```
    ┌─B─┐  ┌─ C ─┐
    (22*2+5)*(3↑2−4)
```

On the next scan, the computer isolates parentheses B, does the arithmetic inside, and the problem is now

$$
\begin{array}{c}
\lceil \text{C} \rceil \\
49^*(3\uparrow2-4)
\end{array}
$$

Since only the C parentheses are left, PET does the arithmetic inside, giving

$$49^*5$$

which after the final multiplication yields the final answer 245.

Thus, if parentheses are nested, PET works back out from the deepest set, working from left to right. When a set of parentheses is removed, the arithmetic operations inside are done according to the order and priority rules already given. A very good rule of thumb for the beginner to follow is that if there can possibly be any confusion about how PET will evaluate an expression, use extra parentheses. Too many cannot harm, but too few certainly can.

One final point about parentheses is that they must be balanced. That is, there must be as many right-opening parentheses as left-opening parentheses. In complicated expressions you should always count the number of right- and left-opening parentheses to make sure they are equal. This doesn't guarantee that the parentheses are grouped correctly, but it will catch obvious errors involving missing parentheses.

E Notation for Numbers

Numbers are printed out by BASIC in different forms. In particular, numbers are sometimes printed out in what is known as the "E notation." Examples of this notation are 2.456E+06 or 6.032E–14. Now we will go back over the ideas introduced in the computer work to clarify the idea of E notation.

It is easy to see why such a special notation is needed for either very large or very small numbers. The PET prints out nine digits in a number, like 1.85369532. A problem comes up if we want the computer to print out a number like 468106327000 which would require twelve digits. PET will print this as 4.68106327E+11, which means that the decimal point belongs eleven places to the right of its present position. A number like 8956000000 would be printed out as 8.956E+09. The E+09 means that the decimal point belongs nine places to the right. We can also express very small numbers in the same way. For example, PET will print out the number 0.000000000683 as 6.83E–10. The E–10 means that the decimal point belongs ten places to the left. The table below should help you understand how to convert from decimal to E notation or from E back to decimal notation.

Decimal Form	E Notation
2630000	2.63E+06
263000	2.63E+05
26300	2.63E+04
2630	2.63E+03
263	2.63E+02
26.3	2.63E+01
2.63	2.63
0.263	2.63E−01
0.0263	2.63E−02
0.00263	2.63E−03
0.000263	2.63E−04
0.0000263	2.63E−05
0.00000263	2.63E−06

To convert from decimal to E notation, count the number of places the decimal must be moved until there is a single digit to the left of the decimal point. The number of places moved is the number that follows E in the E notation. If you had to move the decimal to the left, the sign following E is +. If you moved the decimal point to the right, the sign following E is −.

To change from E to decimal notation, look at the sign following the E. If the number is +, move the decimal point to the right as many places as the number. If the sign after the E is −, move the decimal point to the left.

E notation is not something to get tense about since you will rarely use it when setting up programs on the PET. The main reason for bringing up the issue is that PET may type out numbers in the E notation. Consequently, you should be able to recognize what is happening.

Storing and Retrieving Programs

If every time we turned on the PET, we had to type in the programs that we wanted to use, very little work would get done. One of the nice features of the PET is the built-in tape unit that can be used to store programs. Once we type in a long program and troubleshoot it, we don't want to have to go through the process again every time we want to use the program. Programs can be stored on tape cassettes and subsequently loaded back into PET any time we desire.

Before getting involved in the system commands for storing and retrieving programs on the tape unit, we should pause to consider some fairly obvious facts about tape cassettes. First, if we record a program over a previously recorded program, the original information will be lost. Therefore, if a tape has programs already recorded on it, we must be careful to position the tape so that anything new we want to save will go on unused tape. We will come back to this later. Next, PET must be able to identify a specific program from all the programs stored on a tape. This is done by naming the programs.

To see how programs are stored and retrieved, suppose we have a program entered into PET that we want to save, and its name is TAXES. If you type

```
SAVE "TAXES"
```

PET will respond with

```
PRESS PLAY & RECORD ON TAPE #1
```

At this point, PET is waiting for you to press the PLAY and REC keys on the tape unit. Of course, you should make sure that there is a tape in the tape unit. When you press the two keys, you will see

```
OK

WRITING TAXES
```

If at this point you watch the tape unit, you will see the tape moving, indicating that PET is writing the program on the tape. When finished, PET types out READY.

Now, suppose we want to retrieve the program from the tape. First, clear the screen. Next, clear the program from memory using the NEW command. Then press the REW key on the tape unit, and when the tape is rewound, press the STOP key. Now type LOAD. PET will respond with

```
PRESS PLAY ON TAPE #1
```

When you press PLAY on the tape unit you will see the following:

```
OK

SEARCHING
FOUND TAXES
LOADING
READY
```

It is quite easy to see what is happening by following along the display above as PET locates the program and loads it.

Of course, in this case we had only one program on the tape. A more general situation would involve several programs stored on a tape, with the requirement to load one of them. To see how this would be done, suppose a second program named RATE is written on the same tape containing the program TAXES, and further suppose that the tape has been rewound. If we type

```
LOAD "RATE"
```

and when PET types

```
PRESS PLAY ON TAPE #1
```

we press the PLAY key on the tape unit, we will see the following messages displayed by PET:

```
OK

SEARCHING FOR RATE
FOUND TAXES
FOUND RATE
LOADING
READY
```

In this case we are looking for a specific program. PET identifies each program as it reads through the tape until the desired program (RATE) is located. Then this program is loaded. If a number of programs are stored on a tape, it can take a few minutes for PET to locate a particular program. If no name is specified when the LOAD command is used, PET will locate and load the next program it encounters on the tape.

Finally, if we desire to write a program on a tape that contains information, we should LOAD the last program on the tape. Once this is done we can SAVE a new program and be confident that it is being stored on new tape.

The key to successful program management is to keep track of the programs stored on a tape. With this information in hand, it is easy to position the tape to any desired program, or to position the tape to store new programs.

4-4 PRACTICE TEST

The practice test that follows is provided for you to check how well you have learned the key points and objectives of the chapter. Check your answers against the key given at the end of the book.

1. Write down the symbols that are used to carry out the following arithmetic operations in BASIC expressions: subtraction, multiplication, addition, exponentiation, and division.

2. When evaluating arithmetic expressions, there is a priority of operations. What is this priority?

3. When scanning arithmetic expressions, the computer does the search in a specific direction. What is this direction?

4. Write a BASIC statement to evaluate the following expression. Number the line 100.

$$A = (4 + 3B/D)^2$$

_____

5. If the following program is RUN, what will be typed out?

```
100 A = 2
110 B = 3
120 C = (A*B+2)/2
130 PRINT C
140 END
```

_____

6. Convert the following numbers to E notation: (a) 567300000000 and (b) 0.00000381.

_____

7. Convert the following numbers to decimal notation: (a) 7.258E+06 and (b) 1.437E–03.

_____

8. In the expression below, give the order in which the operations will be done by PET.

```
100 A = (6/3+4)^2
```

_____

9. How do you save a program on the tape cassette?

_____

10. How do you retrieve a program from the tape unit?

_____

INPUT, OUTPUT, AND SIMPLE APPLICATIONS

5-1 OBJECTIVES

In this chapter we will get down to the business of writing programs to carry out tasks. We will also increase our knowledge of BASIC by looking at some details about input and output. The objectives are as follows.

Getting Numbers into a BASIC Program

There are only three ways that we can enter numbers into the computer for a BASIC program. We need to understand how this is done.

Printing Out Variables and Strings

After information is computed, it must be printed out. Different choices are available for how the output is to take place. Usually we will want to output strings of characters as well as numbers. The string output is handled essentially the same way as numbers, but needs special attention.

Spacing the Printout

The previous objective is concerned with the output of numbers and strings of characters. Here we are concerned with the spacing of that output.

The REMark Statement

The wise programmer includes comments in programs to help explain or interpret what is being done. The REMark statement in BASIC permits us to do this.

Simple Applications

Our ultimate goal is to learn how to write and troubleshoot programs. In this chapter we will begin with some modest programming assignments.

5-2 DISCOVERY ACTIVITIES

Let's go straight to the computer work.

1. Turn your PET on and enter the following program:

```
100 INPUT A
110 INPUT B
120 INPUT C
130 D = A+B+C
140 PRINT D
150 END
```

What do you think will happen if we RUN this program?

_____

RUN the program. When the first question mark is typed out (the input prompt for A), type in 2. Likewise, when the second question mark comes up, type in 3, and finally, at the last question mark, type in 5. Record what happened below.

_____

2. Note that in the program in step 1 we have three INPUT statements (lines 100, 110, and 120). Type

```
100
110
```

What does this do to the program?

_____

Type

```
120 INPUT A,B,C
```

Display the program. What has happened?

_____

3. RUN the program, and when the INPUT prompt (?) is output, type in

2,3,5

What happened?

_____

Can you input more than one variable at a time in a BASIC program?

_____

4. RUN the program again, and this time when the INPUT prompt is output, type

2,3

What happened?

_____

What is PET waiting for?

_____

Type

5

and record below what happened.

_____

5. RUN the program, and this time when the INPUT prompt is output, type

2,3,5,1

What happened?

_____

6. Can you type in more numbers than called for at an INPUT statement?

_____

What will happen if you do?

_____

7. Can you type in fewer numbers than called for at an INPUT statement?

_____

What will happen if you do?

_____

8. Type

120 READ A,B,C

Display the program. What has happened?

_____

RUN the program and record what PET did.

_____

9. Now type

125 DATA 2,3,5

and display the program. What has happened?

_____

10. RUN the program and record what happened.

_____

Based upon what you have just seen, anytime a BASIC program contains a READ statement, there must be another type of statement in the program. What is this statement?

_____

11.Name two different methods (other than the assignment statement) for getting numbers into a program. (Hint: See steps 2 and 8.)

_____

12. Display the program in memory. Delete the DATA statement and then type

145 DATA 2,3,5

Display the program again. What has happened?

_____

13. RUN the program and record the output.

_____

Does it appear to make any difference where the DATA statement is in the program?

_____

14. Clear out the program in memory. Enter the program below

```
100  READ A,B
110  C = A/B
120  PRINT C
130  GOTO 100
140  DATA 2,1,6,2,90,9,35,7
150  END
```

What do you think will happen if you RUN the program?

_____

Try it and see if you were correct. Record the output.

_____

Is the "out of data" message associated with the READ statement or the DATA statement?

_____

15. Delete the DATA statement in line 140 from the program. Now enter

```
105  DATA 10,2
115  DATA 100,50
125  DATA 50,5
```

Display the program. What has taken place?

_____

16. If we RUN the program, what do you think will be typed out?

_____

RUN the program and see if you were correct. Record the output below.

_____

17. Can you have more than one DATA statement in a BASIC program?

_____

Does it seem to make any difference where the DATA statements are in the program?

_____

18. Clear out the program in memory. Enter the following program:

```
100 A = 10
110 PRINT A
120 END
```

What will happen if you RUN this program?

_____

RUN the program and record what took place.

_____

19. Now type

```
110 PRINT "A"
```

and display the program. What has happened?

_____

What will happen if we RUN the program?

_____

RUN the program and record what PET typed out.

_____

20. Type

```
110 PRINT "HOUND DOG = ";A
```

and display the program. What do you think will happen if we RUN the program now?

_____

RUN the program and record what did happen.

_____

21. Now let's try a different wrinkle. Type

```
105 B = 2
110 PRINT "B = ";A
```

Display the program and study it carefully. If we RUN the program, what do you think will happen?

_____

Try it and see if you were right. Record the output below.

_____

22. Type

```
95 REM DEMO PROGRAM
```

Display the program. What has happened?

_____

RUN the program. What was output?

_____

Does the REM statement in line 95 have any effect on the program?

_____

23. Clear out the program in memory and enter the following program:

```
100 REM METRIC CONVERSION PROGRAM
110 REM CONVERT LBS TO GRAMS
120 PRINT "INPUT NO. OF LBS.";
130 INPUT P
140 G = 454*P
150 PRINT P;" POUNDS IS ";G;" GRAMS"
160 GOTO 120
170 END
```

Display the program and check to see that it is correct. Study the program carefully and try to guess what will happen if we RUN it. Now RUN the program. When the INPUT prompt is typed out, enter any number you desire. Note what is typed out. Repeat this process several times, then jump PET out of the INPUT loop. Remember that this is done by pressing the RETURN key. What is the purpose of the REM statement?

_____

24. Type

```
115 INPUT P
130
160 GOTO 115
```

and then display the program. What has happened?

_____

Will the program work in this form?

_____

RUN the program and, at the INPUT prompt, type 1. What happened?

_____

Jump the program out of the INPUT loop.

25. Let's experiment with this program a bit more. Clear out the program from memory and enter it again, modified as follows:

```
100 REM METRIC CONVERSION PROGRAM
110 REM CONVERT LBS TO GRAMS
120 PRINT "INPUT NO. OF LBS.";
130 INPUT P
140 PRINT P;" POUNDS IS ";G;" GRAMS"
150 G = 454*P
160 GOTO 120
170 END
```

Can the program be RUN in this form?

_____

RUN the program and, at the INPUT prompt, type 2. What happened?

_____

Explain in your own words what is wrong. Remember that if a variable is not defined initially in your program, PET will set it equal to 0.

_____

26. Jump PET out of the INPUT loop. Clear out the program in memory and enter:

```
100 READ A
110 PRINT A
120 GOTO 100
130 DATA 10,12,9,73,60,82
140 END
```

RUN the program and record what happened. Pay particular attention to the spacing of the numbers.

_____

27. Add a comma after the A in line 110. RUN the program and record what happened.

_____

28. Now replace the comma after the A in line 110 with a semicolon. RUN the program and record what happened.

_____

29. If a variable in a PRINT statement is not followed by any punctuation marks, what happens after the number is printed out? (Hint: See step 26.)

_____

Suppose the variable is followed by a comma?

_____

What will happen if the variable is followed by a semicolon?

_____

30. Clear out the program in memory. Enter the following program:

```
100 A = 10
110 READ B
120 PRINT TAB(A)#B#
130 A = A+10
140 GOTO 110
150 DATA 1,2,3
160 END
```

RUN the program and record what happened.

_____

31. Change the A+10 in line 130 to A+5. RUN the program and record what happened. Again, pay particular attention to the spacing.

_____

32. Now change the A+5 in line 130 to A+3. RUN the program and record what happened.

_____

33. What does the TAB in the print statement appear to control?

_____

34. This concludes the computer work for now. Turn your PET off and go on to the discussion material.

5-3 DISCUSSION

In this chapter we have begun to get away from the mere mechanics of controlling the computer. Instead we will concentrate more on writing and troubleshooting programs. This skill doesn't come naturally to most students, and consequently we will give the topic a great deal of attention, both now and in later chapters.

Getting Numbers into a BASIC Program

In Chapter 3 we saw one way to get numbers into a program. That was by assigning values to a variable in the program itself. For example,

```
100 A = 6
```

introduces the value 6 into a program and stores the number under the variable name A. This method has limitations. We need to examine other ways in which numbers can be introduced into a BASIC program.

Let's look first at the INPUT statement and how it is used. An example might be

```
260 INPUT G
```

When PET executes this line, it will type out a question mark as a prompt that input is expected from the keyboard; it will then halt and wait for you to type in the number. In the case above, the number typed in will be known as G.

More than one variable may be called for in a single INPUT statement, such as

```
420 INPUT A,B,C,D
```

In this case the same INPUT prompt (the question mark) is typed out, but now the computer is expecting four numbers to be typed in, separated by commas. If only three numbers are entered and the RETURN key is pressed, the computer will come back with a prompt for more input since it is still looking for an additional number. If more than four numbers are typed in initially, PET will use the first four as called for in the program, but will warn you that extra input was detected and ignored.

The last method of providing for numerical input into the computer is with the READ and DATA statements. The statement

```
100 READ A,B,C,D
```

is handled by the computer in the same manner as the INPUT statement, with two exceptions. First, the computer does not stop. There is no need to, as will be seen. The second exception is that the numbers called for are read from DATA statements contained within the program rather than being entered at the keyboard in response to an INPUT prompt.

To illustrate the READ and DATA statements, consider the following program:

```
100 READ A,B,C,D
110 E = A+B+C+D
120 PRINT E
130 DATA 25,3,17,12
140 END
```

The program reads four numbers from the DATA statements and prints out the sum of the numbers. It makes no difference where the DATA statement is in the program except that the END statement still must be the highest numbered statement. There can be more than one DATA statement, and they need not be grouped together at the same place in the program. As numbers are called for by READ statements, they are taken in order from the DATA statements, beginning with the lowest numbered statement. Should more numbers be requested after all numbers have been used from the available DATA statements, PET will print out an "out of data" message and halt.

To sum up, there are three methods by which numbers can be introduced into BASIC programs. They are (1) the assignment statement, (2) the INPUT statement, and (3) the READ and DATA statements. There are times when each of these methods can be used to advantage. You will become familiar with the advantages and disadvantages of each method as we spend more time writing programs.

Printing Out Variables and Strings

Output from the computer is quite simple. PET can print out either the numerical value of a variable (a number) or a string of characters. To illustrate, suppose we have a variable named X and the number 2 is stored in that location. The program

```
100 X = 2
110 PRINT "X"
120 PRINT X
130 END
```

shows the difference between string and variable output. Line 110 prints out the character X since X is enclosed in qutoation marks. Line 120 prints 2 since that is the number stored in location X.

You can put numbers in a BASIC program with:
1) LET (assignment)
2) READ—DATA
3) INPUT

The rule is clear. Any characters contained within quotation marks are called strings. Strings are printed out exactly as listed. The computer does not attempt to analyze or detect what is in the strings. If a variable in a PRINT statement is not contained within quotes, PET prints out the numerical value of that varable.

It is possible to do computations within a PRINT statement. Thus

```
100 PRINT A+B+C,D
```

will cause PET to print out the sum of the numbers stored in A, B, and C, followed by the number stored in D. Of course, the variables A, B, C, and D would have to be previously defined.

Spacing the Printout

The PET version of BASIC has a "built-in" standard spacing mechanism that prints four numbers spaced equally on one line. This standard spacing is used by PET when quantities in a PRINT statement are separated by commas. The comma signals PET to move to the next print position on the line. If the computer is already at the fourth position on a line and encounters a comma in a PRINT statement, it does a return and prints the number on the first position on the next line. Thus

```
100 PRINT A,B,C,D,E,F
```

would cause the numerical values of A, B, C, and D to be printed evenly spaced across a line in the four standard positions. The numerical values of E and F would be printed below the values of A and B on the next line.

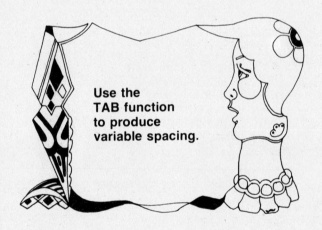

Use the
TAB function
to produce
variable spacing.

Another type of spacing is produced by the semicolon between variables, such as

```
100 PRINT A;B;C
```

The semicolon produces closer spacing than the standard spacing obtained with the comma. However, the spacing is not always uniform, since numbers may be typed out in different formats. We will let it go with the statement that

```
100 PRINT A;B
```

produces closer spacing of output than

```
100 PRINT A,B
```

Finally, we can closely control the spacing on a line by using the TAB function in PRINT statements. The TAB function works in the same way as a tabulator setting on a typewriter. There are forty printing positions on a single line on PET's screen.
The statement

```
100 PRINT TAB(15);A;TAB(32);B
```

signals the computer to space over to the fifteenth printing position, print the numerical value of A, space over to the thirty-second printing position, and finally print the numerical value of B. It is also possible to have a variable tab setting that is controlled by the computer:

```
100 PRINT TAB(X);A
```

Here the computer must first look up the value of X, then space over to the printing position determined by the largest integer in X (for example, if X = 23.1435082, the computer will space over to the twenty-third printing position), then print out the numerical vaue of A.
One final comment about the PRINT statement. We can produce vertical spacing in the output by using a PRINT statement as follows:

```
100 PRINT
```

Since the computer looks for the quantity to be printed and finds none, it then looks for punctuation, and finding none orders a return and drops the cursor down one line. If we wanted two or three empty lines in the printout, we can obtain the vertical spacing by using as many empty PRINT statements as desired.

The REMark Statement

The REM (stands for "remark") statement is quite different from the statements we have seen previously. As soon as PET senses the characters REM following the line number, it ignores the balance of the statement and goes on to the next line. What, then, is the purpose of the REM statement if the computer pays no attention to it? The REM statement is a way of providing information for the benefit of the programmer or someone reading the program. This information makes it much easier to follow what is taking place in the program. The wise programmer will use REM statements liberally.

To illustrate the use of REM statements, two programs will be presented. They both will produce

Put information
in a program
with a
REM
statement.

identical results, but the second uses REM statements to describe what is happening in the program. You can be the judge of which program is easier to follow.

No REM statements:

```
100 INPUT A,B,C,D
110 X = (A+B+C+D)/4
120 PRINT X
130 END
```

With REM statements:

```
100 REM COMPUTE THE AVERAGE OF FOUR NUMBERS
110 REM INPUT THE FOUR NUMBERS
120 INPUT A,B,C,D
130 REM COMPUTE THE AVERAGE
140 X = (A+B+C+D)/4
150 REM PRINT OUT THE AVERAGE
160 PRINT X
170 END
```

5-4 PROGRAM EXAMPLES

As we said earlier, we will spend progressively more time writing and debugging programs. The examples chosen for this chapter are very simple but do illustrate the ideas we have been discussing. Study each example carefully until you are certain that you understand all the details. You might want to enter the programs into PET and RUN them to verify that they work as designed.

Example 1 – Unit Prices

Our problem is to write a program to compute unit prices on supermarket items. We will let T stand for the total case price, N for the number of items in the case, and U for the unit price. We can compute the unit price with the following relationship:

$$U = T/N$$

As an example, suppose that a case of twelve large cans of fruit juice costs $6.96. The unit cost per can would then be

$$U = 6.96/12 = \$0.58$$

We want the program to be designed so that when RUN it will produce the following typical output:

```
TOTAL PRICE? 6.96
HOW MANY ITEMS? 12
UNIT PRICE IS .58
```

The numbers after the question marks are typed in when the program is RUN. For any total price and number of items, the program should compute and print out the correct unit price.

Examine the first line of the desired output. There is a message printed, followed by a question mark and the input of a number from the keyboard. We can do this easily with the following statements:

```
100 PRINT "TOTAL PRICE ";
110 INPUT T
```

Remember that T stands for the total price. The semicolon at the end of line 100 prevents the return of the cursor to the left side of the screen. The next two lines in the program are written in the same style as the first two.

```
120 PRINT "HOW MANY ITEMS ";
130 INPUT N
```

N stands for the number of items. We must now compute the unit price which will be called U.

```
140 U = T/N
```

All that remains is to print out the final line of output, and add the END statement.

```
150 PRINT "UNIT PRICE IS ";U
160 END
```

Now we pull the whole program together.

```
100 PRINT "TOTAL PRICE ";
110 INPUT T
120 PRINT "HOW MANY ITEMS ";
130 INPUT N
140 U = T/N
150 PRINT "UNIT PRICE IS ";U
160 END
```

Study the program to make sure you see the purpose of each line as related to the original description of what was desired. Experiment with various total prices and number of items until you see exactly how the program works.

Example 2 – Converting Temperatures

The relationship between temperatures measured in degrees Fahrenheit and in degrees Celsius is

$$°C = 5/9 (°F - 32)$$

In this expression, C stands for degrees Celsius and F stands for degrees Fahrenheit. If, for example, F is 212, then C is determined to be

$$C = 5/9 (212 - 32) = 100$$

As in the first example, we will write the program after seeing how we want the output to appear. Let's suppose that if we RUN the desired program, we want to see the following typical output:

```
HOW MANY DEG. F
? 212
THAT'S 100 DEG. C
```

Notice that the first two lines of the desired output are slightly different from Example 1. In this case the question mark and input from the keyboard are on the second line. This is accomplished by omitting the semicolon at the end of the first message.

```
100 PRINT "HOW MANY DEG. F"
110 INPUT F
```

Now we compute the number of degrees Celsius using the relationship given above.

```
120 C = (5/9)*(F-32)
```

Finally we print out the last message and the answer.

```
130 PRINT "THAT'S ";C;" DEG. C"
140 END
```

Line 130 illustrates how strings of characters and numeric variables can be printed out in the same PRINT statement. Since C is not in quotes, its numeric value is printed out.

The complete program is listed below.

```
100 PRINT "HOW MANY DEG. F"
110 INPUT F
120 C = (5/9)*(F-32)
130 PRINT "THAT'S ";C;" DEG. C"
140 END
```

As with Example 1 you might want to experiment with this program using different values of F.

Example 3 - Monthly Mortgage Payment

Now let's turn to an example which is more complicated (and also more useful). We want to write a program to compute monthly mortgage payments. The relation to compute this is

$$M = \frac{PI/120}{1 - 1/(1 + I/1200)^{12N}}$$

In this relation P is the initial amount of the mortgage in dollars, I is the annual interest rate in percent, N is the length of the mortgage in years, and M is the monthly payment in dollars. We want the output to appear as follows when the program is RUN:

```
PRINCIPAL ($) = ? 50000
INT. RATE (%) = ? 8.5
TERM (YEARS) = ? 30
MONTHLY PAYMENTS ($) = 384.456734
```

As before, the input from the keyboard follows the question marks and represents a typical case. The monthly payment is shown as PET will print it out. In a subsequent chapter, we will learn how to round off the value to the nearest cent.

By now, the first few lines of the program should follow without difficulty.

```
100 PRINT "PRINCIPAL ($) = ";
110 INPUT P
120 PRINT "INT. RATE (%) = ";
130 INPUT I
140 PRINT "TERM (YEARS) = ";
150 INPUT N
```

Using the values of P, I, and N that have been input, we must now compute the monthly payment. This will be done in three steps.

```
160 X = P*I/1200
170 Y = (1+I/1200)↑(12*N)
180 M = X/(1-1/Y)
```

Study the original expression and lines 160, 170, and 180 until you are sure you understand how the computation is done. The final lines of the program are

```
190 PRINT "MONTHLY PAYMENTS ($) = ";M
200 END
```

The complete program is given below.

```
100 PRINT "PRINCIPAL ($) = ";
110 INPUT P
120 PRINT "INT. RATE (%) = ";
130 INPUT I
140 PRINT "TERM (YEARS) = ";
150 INPUT N
160 X = P*I/1200
170 Y = (1+I/1200)↑(12*N)
180 M = X/(1-1/Y)
190 PRINT "MONTHLY PAYMENTS ($) = ";M
200 END
```

This program has practical value when house hunting. You can quickly determine whether a given house is within your economic means.

Example 4 – Graphic Design

In this example we will create a design using the PET screen as a sketch pad, and then we will capture the design in a BASIC program. You should follow along on your PET.

Type NEW to make sure nothing is in memory. Then clear the screen. Create the design below at the center of the screen. While doing this, use only the blue cursor control keys to move the cursor.

Now move the cursor up to the left side of the screen opposite the top of the design

just created. Type

100 ?"

and press the RETURN key. Recall that the question mark is equivalent to typing in PRINT. What we have done is to capture one line of the screen display in a PRINT statement. Now keep repeating the process using new line numbers until there is a line number opposite each part of the diagram on the screen. Then add an END statement. At this point, the screen should look as follows:

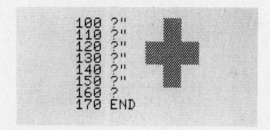

Now if you clear the screen and RUN the program you can watch PET create the design. This example is a very simple graphic application but gives a hint of what can be done.

5-5 PROBLEMS

1. Write a program that will read the four numbers 10, 9, 1, and 2 from a DATA statement, putting the numbers in A, B, C, and D, respectively. Add the first two

numbers, putting the sum in S. Then compute the product of the last two numbers, putting the result in P. Print out the value of S and P on the same line.

2. Write a program that will call for the input of four numbers, then print back the numbers in reverse order. For example, if you type in 5, 2, 11, 12, PET should type back 12, 11, 2, and 5. The program must work for any set of four numbers that you decide to type in. Oh yes, you can use only three lines in your program.

3. What will be output if we RUN the following program?

```
100 READ X,Y,Z
110 DATA 2,5,3
120 T = X*Y+Z
130 S = Y↑2
140 PRINT T,S
150 END
```

4. Explain in your own words what the following program does.

```
100 INPUT A,B
110 S = A+B
120 T = A-B
130 U = A*B
140 PRINT S,T,U
150 END
```

5. If an object is dropped near the surface of the earth, the distance it will fall in a given time can be determined by

$$S = 16T^2$$

where S is the distance (in feet) and T is the time of fall (in seconds). Write a program that when RUN will produce output similar to the following:

```
TIME OF FALL (SEC) ? 2
OBJECT FALLS 64 FEET
```

6. The volume of a box can be computed as V = LWH where L, W, and H are the length, width, and height, respectively. If these are all measured in centimeters,

for example, the volume will be in cubic centimeters. We want a program that will produce output similar to the following when RUN:

```
LENGTH (CM) ? 4
WIDTH (CM) ? 2
HEIGHT (CM) ? 3
VOLUME IS 24 CUBIC CM.
```

The program below is incorrect and will not produce the output called for above. What is wrong?

```
100 PRINT "LENGTH (CM)";L
110 PRINT "WIDTH (CM)";W
120 PRINT "HEIGHT (CM)";H
130 INPUT L,W,H
140 V = L*W*H
150 PRINT "VOLUME IS"
160 PRINT V
170 PRINT "CUBIC CM."
180 END
```

7. In the program below two numbers, A and B, are called for in the INPUT statement. The problem is to supply the missing statements so that when A and B are printed out, the values have been interchanged.

```
100 INPUT A,B
110
120
130
140 PRINT A,B
150 END
```

8. Suppose the odometer on your car reads R1 miles when the gas tank is full. You drive until the odometer reading is R2 at which point G gallons of gasoline are required to fill the tank. The computation to give you the miles per gallon you got on the drive is $M = (R2 - R1)/G$. Write a program to figure out the mileage for the following data:

R_1	R_2	G
21423	21493	5
05270	05504	13
65214	65559	11.5

9. If an amount of money P is left to accumulate interest at a rate of I percent per year for N years, the money will grow to a total amount T given by

$$T = P(1 + 1/100)^N$$

As an example, if P = $1000, I = 6%, and N = 5 years,

$$T = 1000(1+ 6/100)^5 = \$1338.28$$

Write a program that when RUN will produce output similar to the following:

```
PRINCIPAL ? 1000
INT. RATE (%) ? 6
TERM (YEARS) ? 5
TOTAL VALUE IS 1338.22558
```

10. If an amount of money P is left to accumulate interest at I percent compounded J times per year for N years, the value of the investment will be

$$T = P(1 + I/100J)^{JN}$$

Write a program that will call for the input of P, I, J, and N. RUN the program as needed to get the value of $1000 invested at 8 percent for 2 years compounded: a. annually, b. semiannually, c. monthly, d. weekly, and e. daily. If a savings and loan company does a big advertising production about computing the interest every day instead of each week, should you get interested?

5-6 PRACTICE TEST

The practice test that follows is for you to check how well you have mastered the key points and objectives of the chapter. Check your answers against the key given at the end of the book.

1. What will be output if the following program is executed?

```
100 X = 1
110 PRINT X,
120 X = X+1
```

```
130 GOTO 110
140 END
```

---

2. Describe three ways that numbers can be brought into a BASIC program.

---

3. In a PRINT statement, what is a collection of characters between quotation marks called?

---

4. What is the purpose of the REM statement?

---

5. If there is a READ statement in a BASIC program, what other type of statement must also be present in the program?

---

6. What will happen if the following program is RUN?

```
100 X = 3
110 Y = 4
120 PRINT "Y = ";X
130 END
```

---

7. How many standard print columns per line are provided for in BASIC when the print quantities are separated by commas?

_____

8. How many DATA statements may there be in a program?

_____

9. What is the TAB function used for in BASIC?

_____

10. What will happen if the following program is RUN?

```
100 A = 1
110 B = 3
120 PRINT A,B
130 PRINT A;B
140 END
```

_____

11. The program

```
100 INPUT A,B
110 C = A+B
120 PRINT C
130 END
```

is RUN, and in response to the INPUT prompt you type the numbers 10, 12, and 13. Describe exactly what will happen.

---

12. Miles can be converted to kilometers by multiplying by 1.609. Thus, 10 miles equals 16.09 kilometers, and so on. Write a program that will produce output similar to the following when RUN:

```
HOW MANY MILES ? 2.5
2.5 MILES IS THE
SAME AS 4.0225 KM.
```

DECISIONS, BRANCHING, AND APPLICATIONS

6-1 OBJECTIVES

The power of the computer rests in large part on its ability to make decisions about quantities in programs. In this chapter we will explore this capability and will go on with the continuing task of learning to program in BASIC. The objectives are as follows:

Making Decisions in Programs

Decisions made in program can cause the computer to jump to line numbers out of numerical order. Such a transfer to a program line may be unconditional or may depend upon values of variables in the program. The effective use of these conditional and unconditional transfer statements makes simple programs produce powerful and useful results.

Program Applications

As in the previous chapter, we will go on learning how to apply the techniques we study to BASIC programs.

Finding Errors in Programs

Almost all programs have errors in them when first written. Troubleshooting programs is a vital skill that, like programming itself, can be learned.

6-2 DISCOVERY ACTIVITIES

Let's go straight on to the computer work.

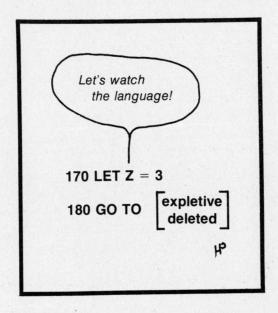

1. Turn your PET on and enter the following program:

```
100 X = 1
110 PRINT X
120 X = X+1
130 IF X < 5 THEN 110
140 END
```

The < symbol in line 130 means "less than"; thus, the statement translates as "If X is less than 5 then 110." Study the program carefully. What do you think will be printed out if you RUN the program?

RUN the program and record what did happen.

_____

2. Now type

$$100 \quad X \; = \; 2$$

Display the program. What will be output now?

_____

RUN the program and write down what PET printed out.

_____

3. Now let's make a few more changes in the program to see if you are following what is taking place. Type

$$120 \quad X \; = \; X+2$$

Display the program and study it carefully. What do you think the program will do now?

_____

Execute the program and see if you were right. Copy below what actually took place.

_____

4. We want to explore another idea in connection with the program you have in memory, but need to make some changes. If desired, you can modify the

program to make it agree with the one below or clear out the program in memory and enter the one below.

```
100 X = 1
110 PRINT X
120 X = X+1
130 IF X >= 5 THEN 140
135 GOTO 110
140 END
```

RUN this program and record what happened.

_____

Compare the output recorded above with that which you copied down in step 1. Is there any connection?

_____

5. In the program in step 4 there is an assertion stated in line 130. The assertion is X >= 5, which is read as "X is greater than or equal to 5." If, for example, X had the numerical value 6, the assertion would be true. If X had the value 3, the assertion would be false. Now suppose we look at the program in step 4. If the program is RUN, the computer starts with line 100, then goes to lines 110, 120, and 130. If the assertion in line 130 is true, which line number will PET go to next?

_____

6. Only two conditions have been used so far in the programs. They are < (less than) and >= (greater than or equal to). How would you write the conditions for "greater than"?

_____

What about "less than or equal to"?

_____

How about "equal to"?

_____

Finally, what about "not equal to"?

_____

If you can fill in the blanks above without too much difficulty, fine. If not, don't worry as we will review everything later. The important thing now is how the IF THEN statement works.

7. Now on to some applications using IF THEN statements. Clear out the program in memory. Clear the screen and enter the following program:

```
100 PRINT "INPUT EITHER 1, 2, OR 3";
110 INPUT Y
120 IF Y = 1 GOTO 150
130 IF Y = 2 GOTO 170
140 IF Y = 3 GOTO 190
150 PRINT "BLOOD"
160 GOTO 100
170 PRINT "SWEAT"
180 GOTO 100
190 PRINT "TEARS"
200 GOTO 100
210 END
```

Display the program and check that you have entered it correctly. Study the program briefly. Remember that when the program is RUN and the computer types out the INPUT prompt, you are supposed to type in either 1, 2, or 3. Which value or values of Y will let the computer reach line 120 in the program?

_____

Which value or values of Y will let the computer reach line 130?

_____

How about line 140?

_____

8. Suppose you wanted the computer to type out SWEAT. What value of Y should be entered?

_____

See if you were right. RUN the program and enter the number you wrote down. What happened?

_____

9. What value of Y will cause the computer to type out BLOOD?

_____

How about making PET type out TEARS?

_____

Check each of the responses you made above to see if you were right.

10. The program assumes that either 1, 2, or 3 will be typed in at the INPUT prompt. Think about the program a bit, then try to figure out what will happen if you type in 4 in response to the INPUT prompt. What do you think will happen?

_____

RUN the program, type in 4 in response to the input prompt, and record below what happened.

_____

You can easily explain what happened in the program by considering what PET does when it encounters an assertion in the IF THEN statement. Remember, if the assertion is true, the computer goes to the line number following the THEN. If the condition is false, the computer goes to the next higher line number. Now jump the computer out of the INPUT loop.

11. Clear the screen and clear the program from memory. Enter the following program:

```
100 A$ = "BLACK"
110 B$ = "WHITE"
120 C$ = "CAT"
130 D$ = "DOG"
140 INPUT X
150 ON X GOTO 160,180,200,220
160 PRINT C$
170 GOTO 140
180 PRINT D$
190 GOTO 140
200 PRINT A$+C$
210 GOTO 140
220 PRINT B$+D$
230 GOTO 140
240 END
```

The program has some new features. First, note that the character-string variables introduced in Chapter 3 are used in the program. The variables are defined in lines 100, 110, 120, and 130. Study the program a few moments to try to see what it does. Now let's try it out. RUN the program and at the INPUT prompt, type 1. What happened?

_____

12. The program is waiting for more input. Type in 2. What happened?

_____

This time, try the number 3.

_____

Enter 4 and record what happened.

_____

13. It should be clear by now that the program is being switched in line 150 to different line numbers depending on the value of X. We have four line numbers in statement 130, and have tried X = 1, 2, 3, or 4. What do you think will happen if we entered 10?

_____

Try it and record below what happened?

_____

We hope that by now you have figured out what is happening. If not, don't fret as we will go over it again later.

14. One last program and we will be finished with the discovery activities. Clear the screen and program. Now enter the following program:

```
100 INPUT A$
110 INPUT B$
120 IF A$ < B$ GOTO 160
130 PRINT B$,A$
140 PRINT
150 GOTO 100
160 PRINT A$,B$
170 PRINT
180 GOTO 100
190 END
```

It is clear that in this program PET will expect character-strings to be typed in at the INPUT prompts. The new and interesting idea in the program is in line 120. Look at this carefully. What do you think the "less than" symbol means with regard to character-strings?

_____

15. Now let's see how the program works. If you RUN the program and at the first INPUT prompt type CAT, and at the second input prompt type DOG, what do you think PET will do?

_____

Try it and record what happened.

_____

16. All right, PET has looped back and is waiting for more input. This time, type in the words APPLE and ORANGE. What happened?

_____

Now try AARDVARK and ARK. Write down what PET typed out.

_____

This exercise opens the door to some very interesting non-numerical applications.

17. Jump PET out of the INPUT loop. This concludes the discovery activities for now. Turn your PET off and go on to the discussion material.

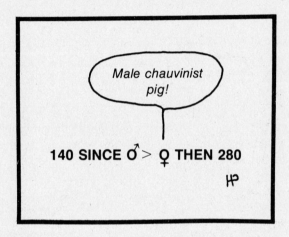

6-3 DISCUSSION

In this chapter we are concerned with two topics. The first is the concept of the transfer statements, both conditional and unconditional, as well as their use in programs. The second topic is the very important skill of troubleshooting and tracing programs.

Transfer without Conditions

From the beginning of this book, we have been using unconditional transfer statements. The following program illustrates the use of the unconditional transfer statement:

```
100 Z = 2
110 PRINT Z
120 Z = 2*Z
130 GOTO 110
140 END
```

Recall that when ordered to RUN a BASIC program, PET goes to the statement with the lowest line number and then executes the statements in increasing line number order. The only way to interrupt this is with a transfer statement (or, as we will see in the next chapter, a loop command). In the program above, the computer would execute line numbers as follows: 100, 110, 120, 130, 110, 120, 130, and so on. The point is that the statement in line 130 causes the computer to jump back to line 110 instead of going to 140. Note that there are no conditions attached to the statement in line 130. This is why the GOTO statement is known as an "unconditional" transfer statement. It is also clear that the GOTO statement puts the program into a loop and there is no way out. The only way we can get the computer out of the loop is to interrupt the program from the keyboard while it is running.

GO TO
is
unconditional.

To sum up, if at some point in a program you want PET to jump to another line without any conditions attached, use the GOTO statement. However, be careful that you don't get the program "hung up" in a loop.

Transfer on Conditions

By now you have most likely established the connection between the IF THEN statements you met in the computer work and the notion of the "conditional" transfer statement. All conditional transfer statements have the same form. A description of this form and a sample IF THEN statement are given below:

Line # IF <(relation)> <(condition)> <(relation)> THEN Line #

```
240 IF 3*X-2 > Y-Z THEN 360
```

All IF THEN statements have this same format. As far as PET is concerned you can substitute GOTO for the THEN. Thus, PET accepts IF GOTO statements but the general format is the same as shown above. The IF and the THEN, as well as the two line numbers in the statement, require no special explanation. However, the heart of the statement lies in the two expressions separated by the condition that forms the assertion. We must look at them very carefully.

In all the examples we have used so far with the exception of the one above, the relations have been either numeric variables, character-string variables, or constants. This is the type of assertion most often used in programs. Examples might be

```
100 IF U < 3 THEN 250
340 IF S$ > T$ THEN 220
```

There are instances, however, in which we might want to use more complicated expressions in the IF THEN statements. In the example following the description of the IF THEN statement, the first relation was

```
3*X-2
```

which is fine providing that X has a value. The second relation

```
Y-Z
```

can also be used if Y and Z have values. To further illustrate what takes place in a program, suppose that X has the value 1, Y is 10, and Z is 4. The computer will translate the statement

```
240 IF 3*X-2 > Y-Z THEN 360
```

y9by first substituting the values of X, Y, and Z. This changes the statement to

```
IF 1 > 6 THEN 360
```

Sooner or later, all IF THEN statements involving numeric variables come down to this form in which the computer must judge whether an assertion established by two numbers and a condition is true or false. If character-string variables are involved, the comparison is done differently, as will be pointed out later. In this case the assertion $1 > 6$ is false. However, an assertion like $4 < 10$ would be true. If the assertion is true, the computer will go to the line number following THEN. If the assertion is false, the computer will go to the next higher line number in the program.

Several conditions may be used in the IF THEN statements. These conditions and their meaning are listed below.

Condition	Meaning
=	Equal to
<	Less than
>	Greater than
<=	Less than or equal to
>=	Greater than or equal to
<>	Not equal to

Multiple Branch Statements

In the computer work we saw that it was possible to branch a program to several different points using only a single statement. Let's use the following program segment to see how this is done.

```
200 ON A GOTO 310,320,330
210 B = A+2
```

In line 200 the decision concerning which line to branch to is based on the value of A. If, for example, A were 1, the program would branch to the first line number in the list. In this case that would be line 310. Likewise, if A were 3, the program would branch to line 330, the third number in the list.

In the example above A should be either 1, 2, or 3 since there are three line numbers in the branch list. You might wonder what would happen if A had some other value. The answer is that when PET is unable to locate an appropriate line number from the branch list, it gives up and goes to the next higher line number in the program. In the example above, this would be line 210.

The ability to control the branching process by changing the values of a numeric variable is the heart of the ON GOTO statement. This multiple branch statement provides a very powerful switching device that has many uses in BASIC programs.

Non-Numeric Branching

As you have seen, we can use character-string variables in IF THEN statements. The comparison between strings of characters is based on the alphabetic position. Thus, A is less than B because A occurs before B in the alphabet. Likewise, Z is greater than T since it occurs after T.

We can extend this idea to words in which case the comparison is made character by character. For example, CAT is greater than CAP. The first two characters in both words are identical, hence no difference is detected in the character-strings. However, on the third character T occurs after P, so CAT is judged to be greater than CAP. In the case of character-strings of unequal length, the comparison is made as far as possible, limited by the length of the shorter character-string. Thus, CAT is less than CATALOG. The comparison is equal for the first three characters (the length of the shorter character-string), but there are characters following this in CATALOG, hence the judgement.

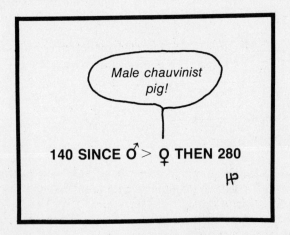

Once this idea of character comparison is understood, character-string variables can be used in conditional transfer statements in the same manner as numeric variables. It should be clear that this capacity to compare character-strings is very powerful and makes sorting and alphabetizing lists of words very simple. We will see several examples of this later on.

6-4 PROGRAM EXAMPLES

Up to this point our programs have suffered from a serious fault. On one hand, the program might involve repetition but there was no way to stop the process. On the other hand, the program stopped but often tended to be trivial. What we want is a way to have the program accomplish a useful task (which may involve repetition) and then shut itself off. The conditional transfer statements just learned provide a mechanism to do this. Now we will look at several programs that illustrate this capability.

Example 1 – Printout of Number Patterns

Our problem is to write a program that will print out the following number pattern when RUN:

```
2       3       4       5
6       7       8       9
```

There are several characteristics of this pattern which we must think about when writing the program. The first number is 2, and succeeding numbers are spaced across in the standard spacing (four numbers to a line). Each number is 1 greater than the previous one. The last number printed out is 9, then the computer should stop.

Several solutions are possible. A program that is not the most elegant but would still work is

```
100 PRINT 2,3,4,5,6,7,8,9
110 END
```

You might check this program to see that it does in fact produce the correct number pattern. It also illustrates a very important concept. There really is no such thing as "the" correct program. The only test that can be applied is "Does the program work?" Certainly some programs are cleverer or may accomplish the results more efficiently than others, but this is a separate issue. The beginner should be concerned with whether or not the BASIC program will produce the desired results, not with questions of style.

Now back to the problem at hand. One way to approach the problem is to make the computer print out the first number in the pattern. We also want to organize the program so that only a single print statement is required. This will require that the program print out the value of a variable that will be changed as the program runs. We can start our program with the following segment:

```
100 X = 2
110 PRINT X,
```

The value of X is set to 2, and this value is printed out in line 110. The comma causes the computer to space across to the next standard printing position. Now we must generate the next value to be printed. Note that at any point in the number pattern, the next number is just 1 more than the present number. This can be done with

```
120 X = X+1
```

Now all that remains is to make a decision about whether or not to loop back to the PRINT statement. As long as X is less than or equal to 9, we want to loop back. We can do this with a conditional transfer statement.

```
130 IF X <= 9 THEN 110
```

The program is finished by an END statement.

The complete program is

```
100 LET X = 2
110 PRINT X,
120 X = X+1
130 IF X <= 9 THEN 110
140 END
```

This program is a simple one and has little practical value other than to illustrate how a conditional transfer statement can get us out of the program at the proper time.

Example 2 – Automobile License Fees

Let's assume that in an attempt to force consumers to use lower-horsepower cars and conserve energy, the state adopts a set of progressive license fees based upon the power rating of the car. The criteria and fees are listed below.

Horsepower	License Fee
Up to 50 hp	$ 0
More than 50 but 100 hp or less	30
More than 100 but 200 hp or less	70
More than 200 but 300 hp or less	150
More than 300 hp	500

We want a program that will produce the following typical output when RUN.

```
INPUT AUTO HP ? 325
LICENSE FEE IS 500

INPUT AUTO HP ? 85
LICENSE FEE IS 30

(etc.)
```

Clearly, the only difficult part of the program will be to decide what the fee is. This decision-making process is made to order for the IF THEN statement. To get started we must provide for input of the power rating. We will use P to stand for the power rating of the car. The program can begin with

```
100 PRINT "INPUT AUTO HP";
110 INPUT P
```

Now we must work out a method to decide in which license category P lies. A logical way to do this would be to check upward from the low horsepower ratings. First, we can check whether P is 50 or less. If so, then we know the tax is 0.

```
120 IF P <= 50 THEN      (fee is 0)
```

The line number following THEN is missing for a reason. If the number in P is less than or equal to 50, we want the computer to jump to a statement that will assign the value 0 to the fee. The problem is that we don't know at this point what line number should be used for this statement. Consequently, we will leave it blank and will return later and insert the proper value. The note after the blank line number is there to remind us of what the fee is supposed to be if the assertion is true and the branch is taken.

If the assertion in line 120 is false, the computer will go to the next higher line number. In that case we want to see if P falls in the next higher category.

```
130 IF P <= 100 THEN        (fee is $30)
```

Again, we don't know what line number to use following the THEN but can fill it in later. There are three branch statements left to determine completely which category contains P. Now that the pattern is established, we can include them all at once.

```
140 IF P <= 200 THEN        (fee is $70)
150 IF P <= 300 THEN        (fee is $150)
160 IF P > 300 THEN         (fee is $500)
```

The program to this point is

```
100 PRINT "INPUT AUTO HP";
110 INPUT P
120 IF P <= 50 THEN         (fee is 0)
130 IF P <= 100 THEN        (fee is $30)
140 IF P <= 200 THEN        (fee is $70)
150 IF P <= 300 THEN        (fee is $150)
160 IF P > 300 THEN         (fee is $500)
```

Now we can fill in the missing line number in line 120. Since the next line number in the program would be 170, we may as well use it.

```
100 PRINT "INPUT AUTO HP";
110 INPUT P
120 IF P <= 50 THEN 170
130 IF P <= 100 THEN        (fee is $30)
140 IF P <= 200 THEN        (fee is $70)
150 IF P <= 300 THEN        (fee is $150)
160 IF P > 300 THEN         (fee is $500)
170 F = 0
180 GOTO        (PRINT statement)
```

Again, in line 180 we have a missing line number. The reminder is that we want to transfer to a PRINT statement. If the assertion in line 120 is true, the computer jumps to line 170 and assigns the value 0 to F, which stands for the fee. We can go on filling in the missing numbers in lines 130, 140, 150, and 160 using the same pattern. The result is

```
100 PRINT "INPUT AUTO HP";
110 INPUT P
120 IF P <= 50 THEN 170
130 IF P <= 100 THEN 190
140 IF P <= 200 THEN 210
150 IF P <= 300 THEN 230
160 IF P > 300 THEN 250
170 F = 0
180 GOTO      (PRINT statement)
190 F = 30
200 GOTO      (PRINT statement)
210 F = 70
220 GOTO      (PRINT statement)
230 F = 150
240 GOTO      (PRINT statement)
250 F = 500
```

The next line in the program would be 260, which we may as well use for the PRINT statement. The rest of the program follows easily. The complete program is given below.

```
100 PRINT "INPUT AUTO HP";
110 INPUT P
120 IF P <= 50 THEN 170
130 IF P <= 100 THEN 190
140 IF P <= 200 THEN 210
150 IF P <= 300 THEN 230
160 IF P > 300 THEN 250
170 F = 0
180 GOTO 260
190 F = 30
200 GOTO 260
210 F = 70
220 GOTO 260
230 F = 150
240 GOTO 260
250 F = 500
260 PRINT "LICENSE FEE IS";F
270 PRINT
280 GOTO 100
290 END
```

You may have noticed that the conditional transfer statement in line 160 is not necessary. To see why, consider the assertions in the IF THEN statements. If the assertion in line 120 is false, we know that P must must be greater than 50. Likewise, if each of the following assertions are false, the computer goes to the next higher line number. In particular, suppose the computer reaches line 150 and determines that the assertion is false. This directs the computer to line 160, but then we know that P must be greater than 300 and can therefore print out the fee without any more testing. If we assign the license fee of $500 in line 160, the result is a slightly different program:

```
100 PRINT "INPUT AUTO HP";
110 INPUT P
120 IF P <= 50 THEN 200
130 IF P <= 100 THEN 220
140 IF P <= 200 THEN 240
150 IF P <= 300 THEN 260
160 F = 500
170 PRINT "LICENSE FEE IS";F
180 PRINT
190 GOTO 100
200 F = 0
210 GOTO 170
220 F = 30
230 GOTO 170
240 F = 70
250 GOTO 170
260 F = 150
270 GOTO 170
280 END
```

Both versions of the program will work equally well, and you may have your own version. How you prefer to handle the branches is a matter for you to decide. The only question to be answered is whether your program works or not.

We have gone through this program in detail because it often proves difficult for the beginner to write programs involving such search rules. You should study the program until you are convinced that it does accomplish what was desired. Also, try to remember to use the technique of leaving line numbers out when you do not know what they should be, then returning later to fill in the proper values. The comments at the right in these cases will help you remember what you want to happen at that branch point in the program.

Example 3 – Averaging Numbers

Suppose we have numbers in a DATA statement which we wish to average. The problem is that we don't know in advance how many numbers there are. So, we will use the strategy of a "flag variable" to mark the end of the data. The flag will be a number that is very unlikely to occur in the data. We will use the number 9999 for our flag, but you could select one of your own choice if desired.

Here is the way it will work. The DATA statement will always appear as follows:

Line# DATA (number),(number),....,(number),9999

The flag 9999 is put in the data after the last number to be averaged. In the program, each time we read a number from the DATA statement we must check to see if it is 9999. If not, we know that the number just read is part of the data to be averaged. If the number is 9999, we know that we have read in all the data and can go on to the rest of the program.

An average is computed by dividing the sum of the numbers by the number of numbers. In our program we must compute both these quantities. We will use S to stand for the sum of the numbers and N for the number of numbers. When the program is executed, we do not know what these values will be, so we must set them equal to 0 and then develop their values as we read in numbers from the DATA statements.

The programs begins by setting up the initial values of S and N.

```
100 S = 0
110 N = 0
```

We really didn't have to do this since PET will automatically zero out numeric variables. However, it makes the program easier to understand if the statements are present. Now we can read a number from the DATA statement and check for the flag value.

```
120 READ X
130 IF X = 9999 THEN        (compute average)
```

We are using the method, introduced previously, of leaving a line number blank in the conditional transfer statement until we know what it should be. In this case, if the assertion (X = 9999) is true, then we know that all the numbers in the DATA statement have been processed and we are ready to compute the average. If the assertion is false, then the number just read must be part of the data and should be processed. This is done as follows:

```
140 S = S+X
150 N = N+1
```

In line 140, the value of X (the number just read) is added to the value in S. Remember that the sum of all the numbers to be averaged is being developed in S. In line 150, the number in N is incremented by 1 to record the fact that another number has been processed.

Having processed the value of X, we loop back to the READ statement to continue the process.

```
160 GOTO 120
```

Now we can fill in the missing number in line 130, since the next line number in the program would normally be 170. In line 170 we compute the average, which we will identify by A. If a typical DATA statement is included, the complete program is

```
100 S = 0
110 N = 0
120 READ X
130 IF X = 9999 THEN 170
140 S = S+X
150 N = N+1
160 GOTO 120
170 A = S/N
180 PRINT A
190 DATA 4,2,3,6,5,9999
200 END
```

Of course, we can have as many DATA statements as needed to hold the numbers to be averaged. Following the last number in the last DATA statement we put the flag 9999 to mark the end of the data. This gets us out of the READ loop and lets us know when to go on to compute the average. The conditional transfer statement, coupled with the idea of a flag variable, gives us a powerful tool to use in programs.

Example 4 – Mortgage Down Payment

The down payment required on a mortgage is determined by the total amount of the mortgage. Suppose a bank has the following set of rules: 5% of the first $25,000, 10% of the next $10,000, 15% of the remainder up to $50,000, and no loans made in excess of $50,000.

Our problem is to write a program to call for the input of the amount to be borrowed, then compute and print out the required down payment. If the amount exceeds $50,000, we will output a message that no loan can be made.

First, let's call for the input of the value to be borrowed.

```
100 PRINT "AMOUNT OF MORTGAGE";
110 INPUT P
```

Now we should check to see that P is not greater than the limit.

```
120 IF P <= 50000 GOTO 150
130 PRINT "NO LOAN ALLOWED"
140 GOTO      (END statement)
```

We will leave the line number blank in line 140 until we know what the line number of the END statement is. The comment at the right is to remind us of where the transfer is to be.

Next, we should check to see if P is greater than or equal to $35,000, or greater than or equal to $25,000. Depending on the outcome we can compute the down payment.

```
150 IF P >= 35000 THEN    (?)
160 IF P >= 25000 THEN    (?)
170 D = .05*P
180 GOTO    (PRINT statement)
```

Notice that if the assertion in lines 150 and 160 are false, we know that P is less than $25,000 and can compute the down payment in line 170. The blank in line 180 will be the line number of the final PRINT statement when we know it. Since the next line would be 190, we can use it for the branch address in line 150.

```
150 IF P >= 35000 THEN 190
160 IF P >= 25000 THEN    (?)
170 D = .05*P
180 GOTO    (PRINT statement)
190 D = .05*25000+.1*10000+.15*(P-35000)
200 GOTO    (PRINT statement)
```

Now we can use line number 210 for the branch address in line 160.

```
150 IF P >= 35000 THEN 190
160 IF P >= 25000 THEN 210
170 D = .05*P
180 GOTO    (PRINT statement)
190 D = .05*25000+.1*10000+.15*(P-35000)
200 GOTO    (PRINT statement)
210 D = .05*25000+.1*(P-25000)
```

The PRINT statement can go in line 220, followed by the END statement.

```
220 PRINT "DOWN PAYMENT IS";D
230 END
```

Now we know that the PRINT statement is line 220 and the END statement is line 230. Putting these numbers in the appropriate blanks, we pull together the complete program.

```
100 PRINT "AMOUNT OF MORTGAGE";
110 INPUT P
120 IF P <= 50000 THEN 150
130 PRINT "NO LOAN ALLOWED"
140 GOTO 230
150 IF P >= 35000 THEN 190
160 IF P >= 25000 THEN 210
170 D = .05*P
180 GOTO 220
190 D = .05*25000+.1*10000+.15*(P-35000)
200 GOTO 220
210 D = .05*25000+.1*(P-25000)
220 PRINT "DOWN PAYMENT IS";D
230 END
```

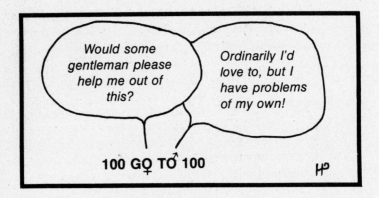

6-5 FINDING ERRORS IN PROGRAMS

The ability to look at a program and determine whether or not it will accomplish what it is supposed to do is certainly one of the most important skills a beginner can acquire. Probably more to the point, when a program is not doing what it is supposed to do, can you find out what is wrong and correct it? These abilities are strange in that until learned, they appear to be very difficult. However, once learned, the programmer usually has great difficulty understanding why everyone doesn't have the same abilities.

Two separate tasks are involved in troubleshooting programs. First, you must be able to translate a BASIC statement into what it means to the computer. Next, you must be able to trace a BASIC program, detailing each step and action as it takes place. We are now far enough into the task of learning about BASIC that we can profitably spend some time on troubleshooting programs. The time spent doing this is golden and will be paid back many times over in time saved in the future.

Translating BASIC Statements

We have been using several different types of BASIC statements. We want to review just what the computer does when it executes these statements. As an example, suppose the computer evaluates the statement

$$140 \quad X = 3$$

This statement instructs the computer to set up a memory location, name it X, and store a 3 in that location. Likewise

$$160 \quad B = 0$$

causes the computer to name a memory location B, and store a zero in that location. The situation is a bit more complicated with the following statement:

$$135 \quad X = A+B-2$$

Now the computer is directed to get the numbers stored in A and B, add them together, subtract 2, and store the result in a location to be named X. This is all right provided that the computer can find memory locations named A and B. If these have not been set up prior to the statement being executed, the computer will search for the locations A and B, and finding none, will set them up, place zeros in both locations, and proceed. Of course this might not be what we wanted at all, so this is something to be careful about.

What happens when the computer encounters a statement like

$$185 \quad IF \quad M = N \quad THEN \quad 240$$

which directs the computer to get the numbers in M and N and see if they are equal? If the numbers are equal, then the next line number to be executed would be 240. If not, the computer would go to the next higher line number. If the computer can't find locations M and N, it will set them up containing zeros. This ensures that the assertion will be true. Again, we must be careful to see that all variables are set up as dictated by the problem or strange things may happen.

Now we want to use the knowledge of how to translate BASIC statements to locate any errors that may be in a program.

Tracing BASIC Programs

The program developed in Example 3 in the previous section will be a good one to use to learn how to troubleshoot. The program is given again below for your reference.

```
100 S = 0
110 N = 0
120 READ X
130 IF X = 9999 THEN 170
140 S = S+X
150 N = N+1
160 GOTO 120
170 A = S/N
180 PRINT A
190 DATA 4,2,3,6,5,9999
200 END
```

The job at hand now is to convince you that the best and most foolproof aid to programming is a blank sheet of paper! Used correctly, this "little dandy" programming aid will enable you to fnd all the errors in your programs and reveal how to correct them. This sounds like a big order for such a simple device as a blank sheet of paper, but it's true! Now let's find out how do do it.

First, copy the program on a lined sheet of paper and follow through our discussion using this copy. Place a blank sheet of paper over everything except the first line of the program

100   LET S = 0

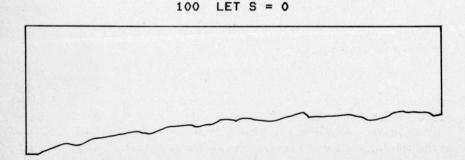

Now we translate the statement, which tells the computer to set up a memory location called S, and store a zero there. We will use our blank sheet of paper to keep track of what is in the computer memory. So we write down an S and underneath place a 0.

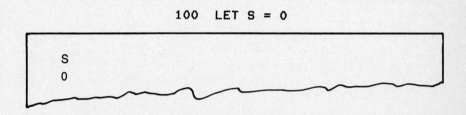

This finishes the first line in the program. Slide the sheet of paper down to reveal the next line and do what is directed. Remember that you are playing the part of the computer and are using the sheet of paper to record what is in the computer memory as well as to let you see only one line of the program at a time.

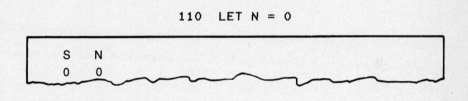

Now on to line 120.

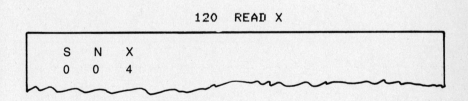

Here the computer is instructed to read a number from the DATA statement in the program, which in this case is 4. The 4 is stored in a location called X.

Let's pause to review what we are doing. We are going through the program one line at a time, writing down what the computer is directed to do. Since we have yet to meet any transfer statements, we simply evaluate a statement, then go on to the next higher numbered statement. Now on to line 130.

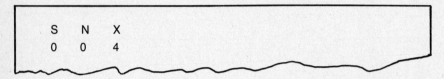

130 IF X = 9999 THEN 170

```
        S   N   X
        0   0   4
```

The assertion in line 130 (X = 9999) is evaluated using the value of X that appears on the paper. Since at this point in the program, X has the value 4, the assertion (4 = 9999) is false. Consequently, instead of going to 170, we drop through to the next line in the program.

140 LET S = S+X

```
        S   N   X
        Ø   0   4
        4
```

We get the number in S (0) and the number in X (4), add them together, and store the sum of 4 in S. Note that this destroys the previous value stored in S. We will simply line out any destroyed value to indicate that it has been lost. At any point in our trace of the program, the value of a numeric variable will be the last number written down in that column. Now the computer goes to line 150.

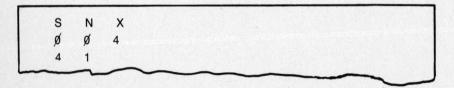

150 LET N = N+1

```
        S   N   X
        Ø   Ø   4
        4   1
```

Here the number 1 was added to the 0 in N, and the sum was then stored in N, destroying the 0 stored there previously. Line 160 directs the computer to go back to the READ statement in line 120. Then the whole process starts again. We stay in this loop until all the data are read in and processed. If you keep tracing the program until the flag 9999 is read into X, your sheet of paper should look as follows:

130   IF X = 9999 THEN 170

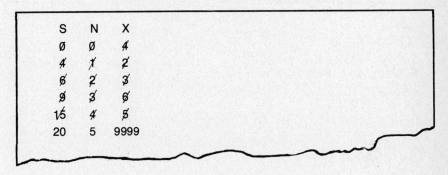

Since the value of X is now 9999, the assertion (X = 9999) is true, and the computer is branched to line 170.

170   LET A = S/N

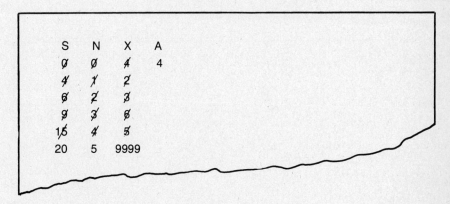

The computer sets up a location called A, divides the number in S by the number in N, and stores the result in A. Finally, the computer is directed in line 180 to print out the value stored in A. Our trace has revealed that the computer is doing what we intended and is producing the correct results.

Now let's look at a program that is incorrect and use the the tracing technique to find out what is wrong. The program is supposed to compute the sum of numbers typed in from the keyboard. Each time PET types out an INPUT prompt (the question mark), we type in one number. When all the numbers are in, we type in 11111 as a flag to indicate that we are through. The computer is then supposed to type out the sum of the numbers entered prior to the flag. The program below is incorrect.

```
100 S = 0
110 INPUT Y
120 IF Y = 11111 THEN 150
130 S = S+Y
140 GOTO 100
150 PRINT S
160 END
```

We will use our little dandy programming aid to find out what is wrong. To test the program we will assume that the following sequence of numbers is typed in as the INPUT prompts are displayed:

3, 1, 6, 5, 11111

The sum of the numbers before the flag is 15, so we know in advance that this is what the computer should print out.

We begin with the blank sheet of paper and the first line of the program,

100   LET S = 0

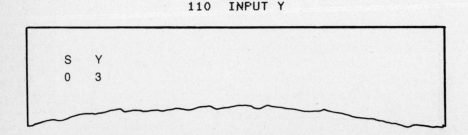

```
    S
    0
```

Then

110   INPUT Y

```
    S   Y
    0   3
```

Since Y is not 11111, we go to line 130,

130   LET S = S+Y

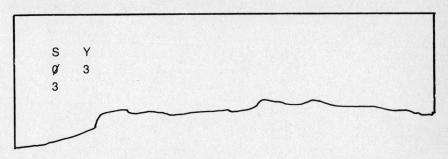

After line 130 we transfer back to line 100,

100   LET S = 0

If you follow the program until the flag 11111 is entered, your sheet of paper should look as follows:

120   IF Y = 11111 THEN 150

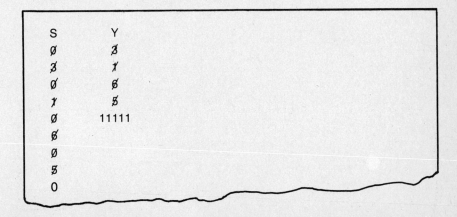

Since at this point, Y contains the value 11111, PET jumps to line 150, which calls for the number in S to be printed out. But the number in S is 0, which is clearly incorrect. If you followed through, tracing the program and writing down all the steps, then you have probably already discovered what is wrong. The error is in the unconditional transfer statement in line 140. With the transfer to line 100, the value in S (which is supposed to contain the sum of the numbers as they are typed in) is set equal to 0 each time a number is entered. The problem is easily corrected by changing the line to

140 GOTO 110

Take the time to learn how to trace programs. If you don't, much time will be lost later on in speculation about what is wrong in your programs.

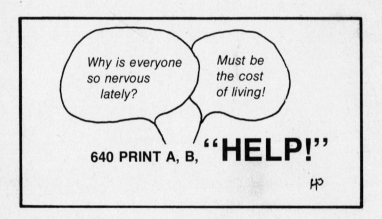

6-6 PROBLEMS

1. Write a BASIC program to call for the input of two numbers. Then print out the larger.

2. Write a BASIC program to READ three numbers from a DATA statement and then print out the smallest.

3. Write a program to compute and print out the sum of all the whole numbers between 1 and 100 inclusive.

4. Describe in your own words what will happen if the following program is RUN.

```
100 S = 0
110 X = 1
120 S = S+X
130 X = X+2
140 IF X < 100 THEN 120
150 PRINT S
160 END
```

5. In Example 3 in this chapter, substitute the following DATA statement:

```
190 DATA 4,2,3,6,5,1111
```

Trace the program by hand and write down what will be output if the program is RUN.

6. Trace the program below by hand using the inputs indicated. In each case, find what will be printed out. The inputs are

a. 1, 2, 3

b. 3, 2, 1

c. 2, 2, 2

d. 3, 1, 3

```
100 INPUT A,B,C
110 IF A < B THEN 150
120 IF B >= C THEN 170
130 D = A+B+C
140 GOTO 180
150 D = A*B-C
160 GOTO 180
170 D = A+B*C
180 PRINT D
190 END
```

7. Suppose you are given a DATA statement that contains a list of numbers of unknown length. However, the end of the list is marked with the flag variable 9999. Write a BASIC program to compute and print out the sum of the numbers in the list between −10 and +10 inclusive.

8. There is an interesting sequence of numbers called the Fibonacci numbers. The set begins with 0, 1. Then each succeeding number in the sequence is the sum of the two previous ones. Thus, the Fibonacci sequence is 0, 1, 1, 2, 3, 5, 8, ... and so on. Write a BASIC program to compute and print out the first twenty numbers in the Fibonacci sequence.

9. Write a program to accept the input of two numbers. If both the numbers are greater than or equal to 10, print out their sum. If both the numbers are less than 10, print out their product. If one number is greater than or equal to 10 and the other is less than 10, print out the difference between the larger and the smaller.

10. An instructor decides to award letter grades on an examination as follows:

$$
\begin{array}{ll}
90\text{--}100 & A \\
80\text{--}\ 89 & B \\
60\text{--}\ 79 & C \\
50\text{--}\ 59 & D \\
0\text{--}\ 49 & F
\end{array}
$$

Write a program to produce the following typical output when RUN:

```
INPUT EXAM GRADE ? 73
YOUR GRADE IS C
```

11. If you use 8 percent more electricity each year, in nine years your consumption will double. Thus, your "doubling time" is nine years. It turns out that there is an interesting rule called the "rule of seventy-two" that can be used to compute doubling times. If a quantity grows by R percent in a single period of time, then the number of periods for the quantity to double is given approximately by 72/R. This is the rule of seventy-two. We can compute the growth of a process directly on the computer. In a single growth period, a quantity Q grows according to the relation

$$Q_{new} = Q_{old}(1 + R/100)$$

Thus, we can keep track of the growth by repeated use of the relation above. When Q is twice the original value, the corresponding number of growth periods would be the doubling time. Using this approach, write a program that will produce the following typical output when RUN:

```
GROWTH RATE (%) ? 3
NUMBER OF GROWTH PERIODS
TO DOUBLE IS 24
```

Use the program to check out the accuracy of the rule of seventy-two for many different growth rates.

12. A set of integers (whole numbers) is chosen at random from the set 1, 2, 3, and 4, and put in a DATA statement. The end of the set is marked with the flag 9999. Write a BASIC program that will compute and print out the number of 1s, 2s, 3s, and 4s in the set. Test your program on the following DATA statement:

```
DATA 3,1,2,14,4,1,2,2,2,3,9999
```

6-7 PRACTICE TEST

Check your progress with the following practice test. The answers are in the key at the end of the book.

1. What will be output if the following program is RUN?

```
100 Y = 3
110 X = 2*Y
120 PRINT X
130 Y = Y+2
140 IF Y <= 10 THEN 110
150 END
```

2. What will be output if the following program is RUN?

```
100 READ X
110 DATA 1,2,3
120 IF X < 2 THEN 160
130 IF X = 2 THEN 150
140 PRINT "GOOD"
150 PRINT "BETTER"
160 PRINT "BEST"
170 PRINT
180 GOTO 100
190 END
```

3. Suppose that you decide to buy a number of widgets. The manufacturer is pushing sales and will give reduced prices for quantity purchases. The price detail is as follows:

# Purchased	Price per Widget
20 or less	$2.00
21 to 50	1.80
51 or more	1.50

Write a program that will produce the following typical output when RUN:

```
HOW MANY WIDGETS ? 40
PRICE PER WIDGET IS 1.8
TOTAL COST OF ORDER IS 72
```

Then keep looping back through the program.

4. Write a program that will print out the number pattern shown below and then stop. Assume that the numbers are spaced in standard column spacing.

```
0          5          10         15
20         25         30         35
           etc.
100        105        110        115
```

5. If you get a ticket for speeding, your fine is based on how much you exceeded the speed limit. The fine is computed as follows:

Amount over Limit	Fine
1–10 mi/h	$ 5
11–20	10
21–30	20
31–40	40
41 or more	80

Write a BASIC program that will produce the following typical output when RUN:

```
SPEED LIMIT ? 45
SPEED ARRESTED AT ? 56
FINE IS 10 DOLLARS
```

SEVEN

LOOPING AND FUNCTIONS

7-1 OBJECTIVES

In this chapter we will learn about two interesting characteristics of BASIC which will provide new and powerful programming capability. The objectives are as follows.

Built-in Looping

We have already learned how to loop programs using either the unconditional or conditional transfer statements. BASIC has special statements to take care of looping automatically. These statements simplify programming and provide flexibility in programs.

Built-in Functions

BASIC contains a number of built-in functions that can be called on to perform specific tasks. We will look at some of the simpler of these functions and see how they can be used to advantage in BASIC programs.

Program Applications

We will continue with activities designed to draw you into programming. Remember that the overall objective of the book is to teach you how to write BASIC language programs for the PET personal computer.

7-2 DISCOVERY ACTIVITIES

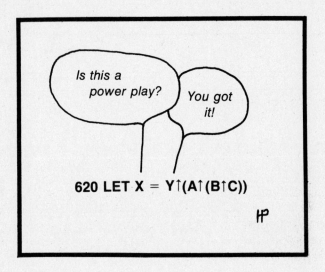

We will go straight to the computer work.

1. Turn your PET on and enter the following program:

```
100 Y = 10
110 PRINT Y,
120 Y = Y+5
130 IF Y <= 50 THEN 110
140 END
```

Study the program and then RUN it. Record what happened.

_____

Which statement in the program determines the difference in the numbers that were typed out?

_____

2. Clear out the program and the screen. Now enter the following program:

```
100 FOR Y = 10 TO 50 STEP 5
110 PRINT Y,
120 NEXT Y
130 END
```

RUN the program and record what happened.

_____

Compare the output with that obtained from the program in step 1.

3. Since the two programs just executed produce the same output, it is reasonable to assume that the statements must be related in some way. Modify line 100 to read as follows:

```
100 FOR Y = 10 TO 50 STEP 10
```

Display the program and study it. What do you think will happen if we RUN the program?

_____

See if you were right. RUN the program and record the results below.

_____

4. Now let's try a few different ideas out on the program. Modify line 100 to read as follows:

```
100 FOR Y = 0 TO 5 STEP 1
```

Display the program. What do you think this program will do?

_____

RUN the program and write down the output below.

_____

5. Now change line 100 to

100 FOR Y = 0 TO 5

Display the program. What do you think this program will do?

_____

RUN the program and record what happened.

_____

Now compare line 100 in the program just RUN with line 100 in the program in step 4. If the difference between the numbers to be printed out is 1, is the STEP part of the statement necessary?

_____

6. Let's try a different tactic. Change line 100 to read as follows:

100 FOR Y = 20 TO 10 STEP -2

Display the program and study it. What do you think this program will do?

_____

RUN the program and record the output.

_____

7. All right, now change line 100 to

```
100 FOR Y = 10 TO 20 STEP -2
```

Display the program. What do you think will happen now if we RUN the program?

_____

RUN the program and write down what happened.

_____

What we have done here is to lead you into a potential trap in BASIC. What seems to be the problem?

_____

8. So far the step sizes in the FOR NEXT statements have worked out without any problems. Let's try a new step size that might not come out even when compared with the limits in the FOR NEXT statement. Change line 100 to read

```
100 FOR Y = 2 TO 9 STEP 3
```

Display the program. Write down what you think will be printed out?

_____

RUN the program and record what happened.

_____

9. We will go on now to some more involved situations involving FOR NEXT statements. Clear out the program in memory, clear the screen, and enter the following program:

```
100 FOR X = 1 TO 3
110 FOR Y = 1 TO 4
120 PRINT X,Y
130 NEXT Y
140 NEXT X
150 END
```

RUN the program and record the output.

_____

10. Now change line 100 to read

```
100 FOR X = 1 TO 2
```

RUN this new program and record the output.

_____

Compare the two number patterns you have just obtained. Can you see the connection between the patterns and the limits in the FOR NEXT statements?

_____

11. Let's modify the program a bit more. Change lines 100 and 110 to read as shown below.

```
100 FOR X = 1 TO 3
110 FOR Y = 1 TO 2
```

Display this program and study it. What do you think will be output if it is RUN?

_____

Try it and see if you were right.

_____

12. One more time. Change lines 100 and 110 to read

```
100 FOR X = 1 TO 2
110 FOR Y = 1 TO 2
```

Display the program and write down what you think will be printed out when the program is RUN.

_____

RUN the program and record the results below.

_____

Clear the screen and LIST the program. Mentally, connect a line from the FOR X statement to the NEXT X statement. Do the same thing for the FOR Y and the NEXT Y statements. Do these imaginary lines cross?

_____

13. Now change lines 100 and 110 as follows

```
100 FOR Y = 1 TO 2
110 FOR X = 1 TO 2
```

Display the program. Now, what do you think will be output by this program?

_____

RUN the program and record what happened.

_____

Clear the screen and LIST the program. Again, draw imaginary lines between the FOR X and NEXT X line numbers in step 12. Do the same thing for the FOR Y and the NEXT Y statements. Do these lines cross? Compare with the same situation in step 12.

_____

Does this suggest a way to avoid getting into trouble using more than one FOR NEXT combination in a single program?

_____

14. In Chapter 5, we experimented with the TAB function to get variable spacing in the output. Now that we have the FOR NEXT statements at our disposal, let's go back to the TAB function. Clear out the program in memory, clear the screen, and enter the following program:

```
100 FOR X = 1 TO 5
110 PRINT TAB(X);
120 FOR Y = X TO 5
130 PRINT "Y";
140 NEXT Y
```

```
150 PRINT
160 NEXT X
170 END
```

Take a few moments to trace the program using the technique developed in the last chapter. Be sure to take the program step by step and write down all the values of the variables in the program as they occur. What output do you think the program will produce?

_____

See if you were right. RUN the program and record the output below.

_____

15. Clear out the program you have in memory. Clear the screen, and then enter the program below.

```
100 INPUT A
110 B = SQR(A)
120 PRINT B
130 GOTO 100
140 END
```

RUN the program and at the INPUT prompt, type 4. What happened?

_____

Now type in 9 and record the results.

_____

One more time. Type in 25. What happened?

_____

Finally, type in 10. What happened?

_____

All right, what happens to A in the expression SQR(A) in line 110 of the program? In other words, what does SQR do?

_____

16. Jump PET out of the input loop. Now change line 110 to read

$$110 \ B = INT(A)$$

RUN the program for the following values of A. In each case, record the output of the program.

A	Output
1	_____
3.4	_____
256.78	_____
0	_____
–1	_____
–2.3	_____

Examine the output you have recorded above and compare each number with the corresponding value of A that you typed in. What does the INT(A) function do?

_____

If you had trouble understanding what was happening to the negative values of A, don't worry at this point. We will review this completely later.

17. Jump the computer out of the input loop. Modify line 110 to read as follows:

$$110 \ B \ = \ SGN(A)$$

Display the program. Review the program structure to refresh your memory about how it works. RUN the program for each of the following values of A. In each case, record the output.

A	Output
1.5	_____
43	_____
128.3	_____
0	_____
−1	_____
−1.2	_____
−345.7	_____
4.7	_____
−5.8	_____

Examine the output above carefully. What does the SGN function do?

_____

18. On to the next function. Jump PET out of the INPUT loop. Change line 110 to read

$$110 \ B \ = \ ABS(A)$$

Examine the program for each of the values of A given below. Again record the output in each case.

A	Output
3.4	_____
0	_____
–3.4	_____
–2	_____
2	_____
–8.45	_____
8.45	_____

Examine the output. What does the ABS function do?

_____

19. Now let's go back to the concept of the character-string variable that was introduced earlier. In particular we want to investigate the characteristics of some functions that pertain to character-strings. Clear out the program in memory, clear the screen, and then enter the following program:

```
100 A$ = "ELECTRONIC"
110 B$ = "CALCULATOR"
120 C$ = LEFT$(A$,5)
130 PRINT C$
140 END
```

The new topic here is the LEFT$ function in line 120. Can you guess what this does?

_____

RUN the program and record what PET typed out.

_____

20. OK, now change the LEFT$ in line 120 to read

$$120 \quad C\$ = LEFT\$(A\$,3)$$

RUN the program and record what happened.

_____

Have you figured out what the LEFT$ function does yet?

_____

21. Let's try this once more. Change the LEFT$ function in line 120 to read

$$120 \quad C\$ = LEFT\$(B\$,8)$$

What will happen now?

_____

RUN the program and see if you were right.

_____

22. Change line 120 to read as follows:

$$120 \; C\$ = RIGHT\$(A\$,4)$$

Now what will be output?

_____

See if you were right. Record the output below.

_____

23. Change the RIGHT$ function to read

$$120 \; C\$ = RIGHT\$(B\$,5)$$

What will PET type out now?

_____

RUN the program and write down what happened.

_____

24. One last function. Change line 120 to read as follows:

$$120 \; C\$ = MID\$(A\$,4,3)$$

You should be able to anticipate what this new MID$ function does. What do you think will happen?

_____

RUN the program and record what happened.

_____

25. Finally, change the MID$ function in line 120 to read

120 C$ = MID$(B$,2,5)

Now what will happen?

_____

RUN the program and record what took place.

_____

26. This concludes the computer work for now. Turn your PET off and go on to the discussion material.

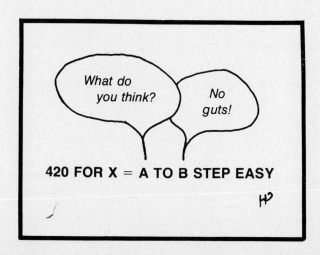

7-3 DISCUSSION

The techniques explored in the computer work can bring new power to the programs we write. We need to understand exactly how these new tools can be used to best advantage.

Built-in Looping

In the previous chapters we learned how to loop programs under the control of transfer statements. The unconditional (GOTO) statement was useful but generally resulted in a loop with no way out. The conditional (IF THEN) statement provided a way to loop the program as desired and also a way to get out of the loop. Both of these are good techniques. However, BASIC has a very elegant way to take care of looping which takes a large burden from the back of the programmer. We will now go over this new method, which uses the FOR NEXT statements.

All FOR statements have the same format. This format and a typical statement are shown below.

Line # FOR $<$variable$> = <$relation$>$ TO $<$relation$>$ STEP $<$relation$>$

```
120   FOR X = 1 TO 9 STEP 2
```

The only things that can change or that are different in FOR statements are the variable and the three relations. If the STEP is left out of the statement, the computer will use a step size of 1. We can write many different forms of the FOR statement. A few are given below to illustrate the range of possibilities.

```
130 FOR J = 2 TO 8
130 FOR T = 25 TO 10 STEP -2
130 FOR W = -20 TO 10 STEP 2
130 FOR X = 3*Z TO A*B STEP D
```

In general, we can write any legal BASIC statement in the relations involved in the FOR statement provided, of course, that the variables used have been properly defined in the program.

The FOR statement opens a loop. We close the loop with the NEXT statement. How this is done is illustrated in the following example:

```
200 FOR X = 2 TO 18 STEP 2   (Opens loop)
                    .
                    .
                    .
            Prosram lines inside loop
                    .
                    .
                    .
340 NEXT X   (Closes loop)
```

In the NEXT statement, the variable must be the same as that in the FOR statement that opened the loop.

It is important to completely understand how these loops work. In the example above, when the computer reaches line 200 the first time, X is set equal to 2. Then the computer works through the lines until line 340 is reached. This closes the loop and directs the computer back to line 200 and the next value of X, which in this case would be 4. The computer stays in the loop until the value of X either reaches or exceeds the limit of 18. Then, instead of going through the statements inside the loop, the computer jumps to the next line number following the NEXT statement used to close the loop. Let's look at an example to see the FOR NEXT statements in action once more.

```
100 A = 1
110 FOR X = 1 TO 6 STEP 2
120 A = 2*A
130 PRINT A,X
140 NEXT X
150 END
```

Since only two variables are involved in this program (A and X), we will list the line numbers in the order the computer encounters them and the corresponding values of the variables.

Line Number	A	X
100	1	
110	1	1
120	2	1
130	2	1
140	3	3
120	4	3
130	4	3
140	4	5
120	8	5
130	8	5
140	8	7 (Jumps out of loop)
150	(Program stops)	

Study the sequence of line numbers and the corresponding values of A and X until you are certain that you understand how the FOR NEXT statements control the loop.

Quite often, more complicated loop structures are required in a program. The structure can be as involved as desired provided that the loops do not cross. The example below illustrates a segment of program with crossed loops.

```
 ┌─100    FOR A = 2 TO 20
 │┌─110    FOR B = 4 TO 8
 ││
 ││       Loops cross!
 ││
 │└─240    NEXT A
 └──250    NEXT B
```

Another example with crossed loops is

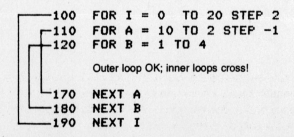

```
 ┌───100    FOR I = 0  TO 20 STEP 2
 │ ┌─110    FOR A = 10 TO 2 STEP -1
 │ │┌─120    FOR B = 1 TO 4
 │ ││
 │ ││      Outer loop OK; inner loops cross!
 │ ││
 │ │└─170    NEXT A
 │ └──180    NEXT B
 └────190    NEXT I
```

The following example illustrates a complicated loop structure in which the loops are organized correctly:

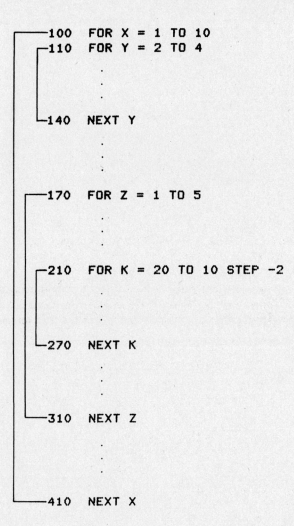

```
100   FOR X = 1 TO 10
110   FOR Y = 2 TO 4
          .
          .
          .
140   NEXT Y
          .
          .
          .
170   FOR Z = 1 TO 5
          .
          .
          .
210   FOR K = 20 TO 10 STEP -2
          .
          .
          .
270   NEXT K
          .
          .
          .
310   NEXT Z
          .
          .
          .
410   NEXT X
```

In this example we have double loops and loops within loops. Remember though, that any combination may be used in a program provided that lines connecting the FOR statements and their corresponding NEXT statement do not cross. If they do, the computer will signal an error and stop.

Don't cross your FOR NEXT loops!

Built-in Functions

One of the advantages of a modern digital computer is that sets of instructions can be preprogrammed to accomplish any desired task. Since there are many computing tasks that are routinely needed, the manufacturers have preprogrammed some of these in the form of functions. With these built-in functions in BASIC, the programmer can perform very complicated operations without difficulty. We will look at several of these functions and see exactly how they work.

Function	Action
SQR(X)	Square root of X
INT(X)	Integer part of X
SGN(X)	Sign of X
ABS(X)	Absolute value of X

Let's use the first function, SQR(X), to see how the functions operate in general. First, X is called the "argument" of the function. If this definition bothers you, then think of X as "what the function works on." If we use SQR(X) in a program, we are instructing PET to look up the value of X, and then to take the square root of the number. For example,

$$SQR(36)\quad = \;6$$
$$SQR(64)\quad = \;8$$
$$SQR(100)\; = \;10$$
$$SQR(2)\quad\; = \;1.41421$$

and so on. The only limitation is that we can't take the square root of a negative number. If the computer tried to evaluate SQR(-6), for example, it would signal an error and stop.

The argument of the function can be as complicated as needed in the program. If the computer runs across an expression like SQR(X+4*Y), it will look up the values of X and Y, carry out all the calculations indicated between the parentheses, and then take the square root. This characteristic is true for all the functions.

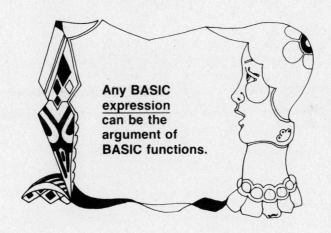

Any BASIC expression can be the argument of BASIC functions.

INT(X) takes the integer part of X. The term "integer" is just a high-class way to say "whole number." Thus, 2 is an integer while 23.475 is not. If we take the integer part of a positive number, we simply forget about everything following the decimal point. Thus

$$INT(3.1593)\quad = \;3$$
$$INT(54.76)\quad\; = \;54$$
$$INT(0.362)\quad\; = \;0$$

However, negative numbers require special attention. What is really happening when we take the integer part of a number is that we go to the first integer less than the number. Using this rule we see that

$$INT(-2) \qquad = -2$$
$$INT(-.93) \qquad = -1$$

and so on. Note carefully that the INT function does not round off a number. Often beginners are somewhat confused about this.

The integer part of a number is the first integer <u>less</u> than the number.

SGN(X) is a very interesting function. If X (the argument of the function) is positive, SGN(X) is +1. If X is negative, SGN(X) is –1. If X is 0, SGN(X) is 0. In effect, SGN(X) returns the sign of X, either +1, –1, or 0. Therefore,

$$SGN(4.568) \qquad = +1$$
$$SGN(375) \qquad = +1$$
$$SGN(0) \qquad = 0$$
$$SGN(-5.9031) \qquad = -1$$
$$SGN(-4) \qquad = -1$$

At this point it may not be clear to you why such a function could be useful. It turns out that the SGN function is very useful, however, and has many applications. For the time being, we will be content just to learn how the function works.

ABS(X) simply tells the computer to ignore the sign of X. In effect, it converts all values of X to positive numbers. So

$$
\begin{array}{ll}
\text{ABS(4.5)} & = 4.5 \\
\text{ABS}(-4.5) & = 4.5 \\
\text{ABS(95.34)} & = 95.34 \\
\text{ABS}(-95.34) & = 95.34 \\
\text{ABS(0)} & = 0
\end{array}
$$

The functions that operate on character-strings are powerful and very useful. The first of these, LEFT$(A$,N), causes PET to select the leftmost N characters in the character-string A$. Of course, any character-string variable can be used in the argument of the LEFT$ function.

To see how the function works, suppose A$ = "HOUSE" in which case

```
LEFT$(A$,2) = "HO"
LEFT$(A$,4) = "HOUS"
```

In the example above, the quotation marks set off but are not part of the substring.

The function RIGHT$ works precisely the same as LEFT$ except the N rightmost characters are picked out. So, if A$ = "TELEVISION" then

```
RIGHT$(A$,3) = "ION"
RIGHT$(A$,6) = "VISION"
```

Finally, MID$(A$,M,N) isolates the Mth through the (M+N)th characters in the character-string A$. If A$ + "AUTOMOBILE", then

```
MID$(A$,2,5) = "UTOMO"
MID$(A$,3,6) = "TOMOBI"
```

There are many other built-in functions in BASIC. However, most of these involve more mathematical knowledge than we can assume in this book. If you have had the mathematics necessary to understand what the functions are doing, you will have no difficulty learning how to use them. If you are interested, consult the PET reference manual.

The built-in functions we have been discussing are used in BASIC statements. Examples of lines that utilize the functions might be

```
100 X = SQR(Y)
100 Z = 3*INT(C)+ABS(D)
```

The built-in functions can be used within functions. An example of this is

```
100 Y = INT(SQR(X)+3*ABS(Z))
```

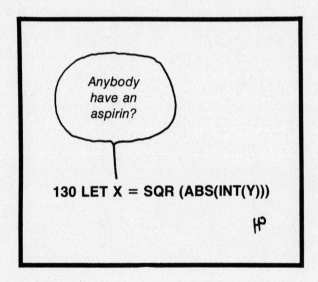

7-4 PROGRAM EXAMPLES

The example programs that we will study have been chosen to show you how we can use automatic looping and the built-in functions to make programming easier.

Example 1 - Finding an Average

In the previous chapter, we used the problem of finding an average for one of the example programs. Let's return to the same problem, but use a different method. We want the program to produce printout similar to the following when RUN:

```
HOW MANY NUMBERS ? 5
ENTER THE NUMBERS,
ONE AT A TIME
? 12.5
? 10.8
? 11.3
? 14.1
? 12.8
THE AVERAGE IS 12.3
```

The first few lines should be easy for you to write by now.

```
100 PRINT "HOW MANY NUMBERS";
110 INPUT N
120 PRINT "ENTER THE NUMBERS,"
130 PRINT "ONE AT A TIME"
```

Now we must arrange for the input of N numbers but must also keep in mind that we are supposed to compute the average of the numbers. So initially we will set S (which will be used to sum the numbers) equal to 0.

```
140 S = 0
```

The input of N numbers and the summing up of them is an ideal task for the FOR NEXT statements.

```
150 FOR I = 1 TO N
160 INPUT X
170 S = S+X
180 NEXT I
```

Notice that we don't use I, the loop variable, except to count the numbers as they are input. When all the numbers are in, the computer will jump out of the loop to the next higher line number after 180. When this happens, S will contain the sum of all the values of X that were typed in. Since we know that N is the number of numbers typed in, we can immediately compute the average.

```
190 A = S/N
```

The rest of the program follows without difficulty.

```
200 PRINT "THE AVERAGE IS";A
210 END
```

The complete program is

```
100 PRINT "HOW MANY NUMBERS";
110 INPUT N
120 PRINT "ENTER THE NUMBERS,"
130 PRINT "ONE AT A TIME"
140 S = 0
150 FOR I = 1 TO N
160 INPUT X
170 S = S+X
180 NEXT I
190 A = S/N
200 PRINT "THE AVERAGE IS";A
210 END
```

Example 2 – Temperature Conversion Table

In one of the earlier programs we used the relation

$$C = 5/9 \, (F - 32)$$

to convert from degrees Fahrenheit to degrees Celsius. Now let's generate a conversion table as follows:

Degrees F	Degrees C
0	−17.7777
5	−15
10	−12.2222
etc.	
100	37.7777

First we should print out the heading and the space before beginning the table itself.

```
100 PRINT "DEG. F","DEG. C"
110 PRINT
```

We can use a FOR NEXT loop to generate the values of F, which can then be converted to C and printed out.

```
120 FOR F = 0 TO 100 STEP 10
130 C = 5*(F-32)/9
140 PRINT F,C
150 NEXT F
```

Finally, we need the END statement.

```
160 END
```

The whole program is given below.

```
100 PRINT "DEG. F","DEG. C"
110 PRINT
120 FOR F = 0 TO 100 STEP 5
130 C = 5*(F-32)/9
140 PRINT F,C
150 NEXT F
160 END
```

Example 3 – An Alphabet Problem

Suppose we want to write a program to print out the pattern shown below.

```
ABCDEF
BCDEFG
CDEFGH
 etc.
```

The pattern should continue until we have run through the complete alphabet. We will need a character-string function to do this. First, however, we will set up a character-string to define the alphabet.

```
100 A$ = "ABCDEFGHIJKLMNOPQRSTUVWXYZ"
```

If you look carefully at the desired pattern, you will see that twenty-one lines will have to be printed out. Each line will have six characters. We will have to arrange to print each line one space further to the right than the previous one.

The commands necessary to do this are

```
110 FOR I = 1 TO 21
120 PRINT TAB(I);
130 PRINT MID$(A$,I,6)
140 NEXT I
```

The printing is positioned by the TAB function in line 120. Groups of six characters are picked out by the MID$ function in line 130.

After adding the END statement, the complete program is

```
100 A$ = "ABCDEFGHIJKLMNOPQRSTUVWXYZ"
110 FOR I = 1 TO 21
120 PRINT TAB(I);
130 PRINT MID$(A$,I,6)
140 NEXT I
150 END
```

This is a good program to experiment with. First, RUN the program to see that you do get the correct letter pattern. Then, you might want to change some of the parameters in the program and see what happens.

Example 4 - Depreciation Schedule

When a company invests in equipment, the investment is depreciated over a number of years for tax purposes. This means that the value of the equipment is decreased each year (due to use, wear, and tear), and the amount of decrease is a tax-deductible item. One of the methods used to compute depreciation is the "sum-of-the-years-digits" schedule.

To illustrate, suppose a piece of equipment has a lifetime of five years. The sum of the years digits would be

$$1 + 2 + 3 + 4 + 5 = 15$$

The depreciation the first year will be 5/15 of the initial value; the depreciation fraction the second year will be 4/15; and so on. Each year the value of the equipment is decreased by the amount of the depreciation. At the end of the last year's useful life, the equipment's value will be zero.

We want to write a BASIC program to generate depreciation schedules. First, we must know what the value of the equipment is, and its useful lifetime.

```
100 PRINT "ASSET VALUE ($)";
110 INPUT P
120 PRINT "ASSET LIFE (YEARS)";
130 INPUT N
140 PRINT
```

Next, we can print out the column headings for the table.

```
150 PRINT "YEAR","DEPREC.","VALUE"
160 PRINT
```

The sum-of-the-years-digits is computed easily.

```
170 S = 0
180 FOR I = 1 TO N
190 S = S+I
200 NEXT I
```

Now we compute the schedule and print it out. We will use the variable P1 to keep track of the current asset value.

```
220 P1 = P
230 FOR I = 1 TO N
240 F = (N+1-I)/S
250 D = P*F
260 P1 = P1-D
270 PRINT I,D,P1
280 NEXT I
```

In line 240, F is the depreciation fraction for the Ith year. You can check this out for various values of I to ensure that the expression does generate the correct value of F. In line 250, D is the depreciation. The only thing mising now is the END statement. The complete program is

```
100 PRINT "ASSET VALUE ($)";
110 INPUT P
120 PRINT "ASSET LIFE (YEARS)";
130 INPUT N
140 PRINT
150 PRINT "YEAR","DEPREC.","VALUE"
160 PRINT
170 S = 0
180 FOR I = 1 TO N
190 S = S+I
200 NEXT I
220 P1 = P
230 FOR I = 1 TO N
240 F = (N+1-I)/S
250 D = P*F
260 P1 = P1-D
270 PRINT I,D,P1
280 NEXT I
290 END
```

Try out the program for different inputs. Of course, you can use this program to set up schedules to be used on your tax returns. Impress the Internal Revenue Service with your PET-generated depreciation schedules!

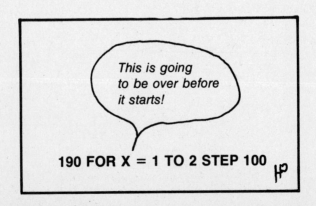

This is going to be over before it starts!

190 FOR X = 1 TO 2 STEP 100

7-5 PROBLEMS

1. Write a program to generate a table of numbers and their square roots. The table should look as follows:

N	SQR(N)
2.0	1.41421
2.1	1.44914
2.2	1.48324
etc.	
3.9	1.97484
4.0	2.00000

2. The problem is to evaluate the expression

$$X^2 + 3X - 4$$

for X = 0, 0.1, 0.2, ..., 1.9, 2.0. Print out the values of X and the corresponding values of the expression on the same line.

3. Write a program to accept the input of a number N, then print out the even numbers greater than 0, but less than or equal to N.

4. Write a program using FOR NEXT statements to read ten pairs of numbers from DATA statements. For each pair, print out the numbers and their sum.

5. Trace the following program. What will be output if it is RUN?

```
100 FOR I = 1 TO 5
110 READ A
120 B = INT(A)-SGN(A)*2
130 PRINT B
140 NEXT I
150 DATA 2.2,-3,10,0,-1.5
160 END
```

6. Explain what the following program does:

```
100 FOR X = 1 TO 5
110 READ Y
120 Z = INT(100*Y+.5)/100
130 PRINT Z
140 NEXT X
150 DATA 1.06142,27.5292,138.021
160 DATA .423715,51.9132
170 END
```

7. N! is read "N factorial" and means the product of all the whole numbers from 1 to N inclusive. For example

$$3! = (1)(2)(3) = 6$$
$$5! = (1)(2)(3)(4)(5) = 120$$

and so on. Write a program to call for the input of N. Then compute and print out N! If you try out this program on the PET, you may be surprised to find that values of N that don't seem large at all to you produce factorials too large to handle. The factorial of N is an extremely rapidly increasing function.

8. Write a BASIC program to call for N grades to be input. Compute and print out (1) the highest grade, (2) the lowest grade, and (3) the average of the grades.

9. What, if anything is wrong with the following program?

```
100 FOR X = 1 TO 2
110 FOR Y = 2 TO 6
120 PRINT X+Y
130 NEXT Y
140 FOR Z = 1 TO 3
150 PRINT X+Z
160 NEXT X
170 NEXT Z
180 END
```

10. What will be output if the following program is RUN?

```
100 FOR X = 1 TO 4
110 FOR Y = 1 TO 3
120 Z = X*Y
130 PRINT Z,
140 NEXT Y
150 PRINT
160 NEXT X
170 END
```

11. Suppose you decide to invest $1000 on the first day of each year for 10 years at an annual simple interest rate of 6 percent. At the end of the tenth year, the value of the investment will be $13,971.64. To see how this could be computed, use the following formula:

$$P2 = (P1+I) (1+R/100)$$

In this formula, R is the annual interest rate in percent, I is the annual investment in dollars, P1 is the value of the investment at the beginning of each year, and P2 is the value of the investment at the end of the year. Thus, P2 becomes P1 for the next year. Write a BASIC program which will produce the following typical output when RUN:

```
ANNUAL INVESTMENT ? 1000
INTEREST RATE (%) ? 8
HOW MANY YEARS ? 20
AT THE END OF THE
LAST YEAR, THE VALUE
OF THE INVESTMENT
WILL BE 49422.9215
```

12. The DATA statements below contain the time worked by a number of employees during a one-week period.

```
190 DATA 5
200 DATA 2,4.8,8,10,8,7,10
201 DATA 5,3.75,7,8,8,6,10
202 DATA 1,3.25,8,10,6,8,8
203 DATA 4,5.8,10,6,10,6
204 DATA 3,4.25,6,6,8,10,7
```

The number in line 190 gives the number of employees to follow. Each of the DATA lines after 190 contains a weekly record for one employee. The data are an employee number, the hourly rate, and the hours worked Monday through Friday. The employee receives time and a half for everything over 40 hours per week. Write a BASIC program using these DATA statements to compute and print out the employee number and the gross pay for the week for each of the employees.

13. Assume that the following DATA statements give the performance of the students in an English class on three examinations:

```
190 DATA 6
200 DATA 3,90,85,92
201 DATA 1,75,80,71
202 DATA 6,100,82,81
203 DATA 5,40,55,43
204 DATA 2,60,71,68
205 DATA 4,38,47,42
```

The number in line 190 is the number of students in the class. Each of the DATA statements that follow gives the performance for a single student. The information is the student ID number, grade 1, grade 2, and grade 3. Thus as shown in line 202, student 6 got examination grades of 100, 82, and 81. Write a program using these DATA statements to compute and print out each student's ID number and his or her course grade. Assume that the first two examination grades are weighted 25% each toward the overall grade and the last grade is weighted 50%.

7-6 PRACTICE TEST

See how well you have learned the material in the chapter by taking this practice test. The answers are given at the end of the book.

1. What will be printed if the following program is RUN?

```
100 FOR Y = 20 TO 1 STEP -2
110 PRINT Y,
120 NEXT Y
130 END
```

2. What will be printed if the following program is RUN?

```
100 FOR A = 1 TO 4
110 FOR B = 1 TO 3
120 PRINT A*B
130 NEXT B
140 NEXT A
150 END
```

3. Fill in the blanks.

a. SQR(36) =   _____

b. INT(7.13) =   _____

c. ABS(−22.8) =   _____

d. SGN(−1.3) =   _____

4. What (if anything) is wrong with the following program?

```
100 FOR I = 1 TO 5
110 FOR J = 2 TO 5
120 PRINT I,J
130 NEXT I
140 NEXT J
150 END
```

5. Miles can be converted to kilometers by multiplying the number of miles by 1.609. Write a program to produce a table similar to the following:

Miles	Kilometers
10	16.09
15	24.135
20	32.18
etc.	
100	160.9

6. Numerical information is loaded into DATA statements as follows:

```
100 DATA 10
110 DATA 25,21,24,21,26,27,25,24,23,24
```

The number in line 100 gives the number of numbers to be processed in the rest of the DATA statements. Write a program using these statements to compute the average of the numbers excluding the one in line 100.

EIGHT

WORKING WITH COLLECTIONS OF INFORMATION

8-1 OBJECTIVES

In this chapter we will apply some of the ideas learned earlier to collections of information. New concepts will be introduced which will expand the capability of BASIC. The objectives are as follows.

Subscripted String Variables

The notion of a character-string variable can be extended to subscripted character-strings. This capability makes powerful non-numeric applications possible.

Single and Double Subscripted Numeric Variables

Much more powerful programs dealing with numbers can be written using subscripted numeric variables. Therefore we will see what subscripted numeric variables are and how to use them.

Program Applications

We will study BASIC programs that take advantage of both subscripted numeric variables, and subscripted character-string variables.

8-2 DISCOVERY ACTIVITIES

Since beginners often tend to have difficulty with this material, some introduction is needed before the computer work is started.

When working with groups of information we must be able to distinguish members of the group from one another. This the reason for subscripts. Before getting into subscripts, however, we need to add two important words to our computer vocabulary. We could use the word "collection" to describe a group of pieces of information, but it turns out that two other words are more commonly used. The words are "matrix" and "array." For our purposes they both mean the same thing: a "collection of pieces of information." If you had seen the terms matrix and array before understanding a little about what the words mean, you might have gotten unnecessarily excited. Remember, then, the terms matrix and array mean a collection of information. The pieces of information in the collection can be either numeric or character-string.

To see how this works, let's look at the array given below.

$$Y(1) = 9$$
$$Y(2) = 10$$
$$Y(3) = 7$$
$$Y(4) = 14$$
$$Y(5) = 12$$
$$Y(6) = 15$$

The name of this numeric array is Y. Its size is six, since there are six "elements" or "members" in the array. The numers 9, 10, 7, 14, 12, and 15 are the elements in the array. The numbers printed in parentheses to the right of the Ys are called "subscripts." Each subscript points to one element in the array. Thus, Y(4) means the fourth number in the array, which is this case is 14. We read Y(4) as "Y sub four." The third number in the array would be called "Y sub three," and so on. This array is one-dimensional, since it takes only a single number (or subscript) to locate a given element in the array.

Now, let's look at a more complicated example but one which still uses the ideas introduced above.

$$Z\$(1,1) = \text{"DOG"} \qquad Z\$(1,2) = \text{"ON"} \qquad Z\$(1,3) = \text{"NOTE"}$$
$$Z\$(2,1) = \text{"BUT"} \qquad Z\$(2,2) = \text{"RED"} \qquad Z\$(2,3) = \text{"NOT"}$$

In this example there are six elements in the character-string array Z\$. Since it is a character-string array, the elements of Z\$ are words. However, this is a two-dimensional array, since we must specify which row and column we want. The first subscript gives the row number; the second specifies the column. $Z\$(2,1)$ is read as "Z string sub two one" and means the element of Z\$ found in the second row and first column. In this case, $Z\$(2,1)$ is the word "BUT." Likewise, $Z\$(1,3)$ is "NOTE," and so on.

To sum up, we will work with two kinds of matrices or arrays. The one-dimensional array needs only a single number to locate an element in that array. The two-dimensional array needs two numbers (a row number and a column number) to locate an element. Both one- or two-dimensional arrays can be either numeric or character-string. The one-dimensional array is associated with the idea of a single-subscripted variable. Likewise, the double-subscripted variable is used in the two-dimensional array. With this brief introduction, you are ready for the computer work.

MATRIX and ARRAY
mean
collections
of numbers.

1. Turn your PET on, and enter the following program:

```
100 A$(1) = "HOUSE"
110 A$(2) = "BARN"
120 A$(3) = "SHED"
130 A$(4) = "STORE"
140 A$(5) = "CABIN"
150 PRINT A$(4)
160 END
```

What do you think will be printed out if we RUN this program?

_____

RUN the program and record what happened.

_____

2. OK, change line 150 to read

```
150 PRINT A$(1),A$(3)
```

Now what do you think will happen?

_____

RUN the program and write down what PET printed out.

_____

3. Change the comma in line 150 to a + so that the line now reads

        150 PRINT A$(1)+A$(3)

RUN the program and record what happened.

_____

What does the + do when printing out character-strings?

_____

4. Clear the program from memory, and clear the screen. Enter the following program:

```
100 FOR I = 1 TO 5          '
110 READ B$(I)
120 NEXT I
130 DATA "RED","WHITE","BLUE"
140 DATA "GREEN","BROWN"
150 PRINT B$(3)
160 END
```

Study the program for a few moments. What do you think will be printed out if the program is RUN?

_____

RUN the program and see if you were right.

_____

5. Delete lines 150 and 160 from the program. Enter the following additions:

```
150 FOR I = 1 TO 5
160 PRINT B$(I),
170 NEXT I
180 END
```

Now what do you think will happen?

_____

RUN the program and record what PET did.

_____

6. Change line 150 to read

```
150 FOR I = 5 TO 1 STEP -2
```

RUN the program and write down the output.

_____

7. Now let's extend the subject a bit. Clear out the program in memory and enter the following:

```
100 C$(1,1) = "WHITE"
110 C$(1,2) = "BLACK"
```

```
120 C$(1,3) = "BROWN"
130 C$(2,1) = "CAR"
140 C$(2,2) = "BIKE"
150 C$(2,3) = "PLANE"
160 FOR I = 1 TO 2
170 PRINT C$(I,2)
180 NEXT I
190 END
```

This program is more complicated but you should be able to figure out what it does. RUN the program and record what took place.

_____

8. OK, change line 170 to read

```
170 PRINT C$(I,3)
```

What will be output now?

_____

RUN the program and record what happened.

_____

9. Change lines 160, 170, and 180 to read

```
160 FOR J = 1 TO 3
170 PRINT C$(1,J)
180 NEXT J
```

What will the program do now?

_____

RUN the program and record the output.

_____

10. Change line 170 to read

```
170 PRINT C$(2,J)
```

Now what will be output?

_____

RUN the program and write down what took place.

_____

11. So far we have been working with collections of words. We can work equally well with collections of numbers. Clear the program from memory and enter the following:

```
100 X(1) = 21
110 X(2) = 13
120 X(3) = 16
130 X(4) = 8
140 X(5) = 11
150 PRINT X(1)
160 END
```

What do you think will happen if we RUN this program?

_____

RUN the program and record what happened.

_____

12. Now modify the program to print out the fourth value of X. RUN the program. Did it work?

_____

13. OK, change line 150 as follows:

```
150 PRINT X(3)+X(4)
```

Display the program and study it briefly. What do you think will happen if we RUN the program?

_____

RUN the program and see if you were right. Record below what actually was printed out.

_____

14. Type

```
150 FOR I = 1 TO 5
152 PRINT X(I)
154 NEXT I
```

Display the program. What do you think will be printed out by this program?

_____

See if you were right. Record below what happened when the program was RUN.

_____

15. Modify this program to print out only the first three values of the array X. Record below what happened when you tried this.

_____

16. Again, modify the program, but this time so that the first value of the array, and then every other value, will be printed out. Record what happened below.

_____

17. Clear out the program in memory. Enter the following program:

```
100 Y(1,1) = 2
110 Y(1,2) = 5
120 Y(1,3) = 1
130 Y(2,1) = 2
140 Y(2,2) = 4
150 Y(2,3) = 3
160 PRINT Y(1,3)
170 END
```

Display the program and make sure you have entered it correctly. What do you think this program does?

_____

RUN the program and record what was printed out.

_____

18. Type

```
160 PRINT Y(2,2)+Y(1,3)+Y(1,1)
```

Display the program. What will this program do?

_____

RUN the program and see if you were right.

_____

19. Type

```
160 S = 0
162 FOR J = 1 TO 3
164 S = S+Y(1,J)
166 NEXT J
168 PRINT S
```

Display the program and study it carefully. What will happen if we RUN this program?

_____

RUN the program and record what was printed out.

_____

Explain in your own words what is taking place in the program.

_____

20. Type

```
162 FOR I = 1 TO 2
164 S = S+Y(I,2)
166 NEXT I
```

Display the program. What is the program doing now?

_____

RUN the program and write down what was printed out.

_____

Again try to explain in your own words what is happening.

_____

21. Now type

```
162 FOR I = 1 TO 2
164 FOR J = 1 TO 3
166 S = S+Y(I,J)
168 NEXT J
170 NEXT I
172 PRINT S
180 END
```

Display the program and think a minute about it. In particular, compare what you see now with what was going on in steps 19 and 20. What does this program do?

_____

RUN the program and record what was typed out.

_____

22. Clear out the program in memory. Enter the following program:

```
100 DIM X(12),Y(12)
110 FOR I = 1 TO 12
```

```
120 READ X(I),Y(I)
130 NEXT I
140 PRINT X(1)+Y(4)
150 DATA 2,1
151 DATA -1,3
152 DATA 5,6
153 DATA 2,4
154 DATA 3,1
155 DATA 8,4
156 DATA 5,1
157 DATA 3,4
158 DATA 6,2
159 DATA 1,1
160 DATA 7,7
161 DATA 5,3
170 END
```

Display the program and check to see that you have entered it correctly. Study the program carefully. If we RUN the program, what will be typed out?

_____

RUN the program and see whether or not you were right. Record below what was typed out.

_____

23. Type

100

Now display the program. What has happened?

_____

RUN the program and record what happened.

_____

Does the DIM statement that was originally present in the program appear to be necessary?

_____

24. Type

```
100 DIM X(9),Y(9)
110 FOR I = 1 TO 9
```

Display the program. What will happen now if we RUN the program?

_____

Try it and see if you were correct.

_____

25. Type

```
100
```

Doing this deleted line 100 from the program. Will the program work now that the DIM statement has been taken out?

_____

Try it and record the output.

_____

Compare the results of step 23 with those of step 25. Sometimes the DIM statement must be present and other times it need not be. We will return to this question later.

26. Clear out the program in memory. Enter the following program:

```
100 DIM A(4,3)
110 FOR I = 1 TO 4
120 FOR J = 1 TO 3
130 READ A(I,J)
140 NEXT J
150 NEXT I
160 FOR I = 1 TO 4
170 FOR J = 1 TO 3
180 PRINT A(I,J);
190 NEXT J
200 PRINT
210 PRINT
220 NEXT I
230 DATA 1,3,1
240 DATA 4,2,5
250 DATA 1,4,2
260 DATA 3,2,5
270 END
```

Make sure that you have entered the program correctly, then take a few minutes to study it. Can you see what will be printed out if we execute the program?

_____

RUN the program and record the output.

_____

Compare what was printed out with the numbers in the DATA statements in the program.

27. This concludes the computer work for now. Turn your PET off and go on to the discussion material.

8-3 DISCUSSION

It is natural to be a bit confused at this point about arrays, both numeric and string. Therefore it is important that you pay particular attention to the discussion material to clear up any questions that might have arisen in the computer work.

Single and Double Subscripted Variables

The need for subscripted variables becomes obvious when we must handle large collections of information. It makes no difference whether the information is string or numeric. If, for example, we were writing a program that involved only four numbers, we would have no difficulty naming them. We might call the numbers X, Y, U, and V. But suppose we needed to work with 100 numbers? For this, and other reasons, it is often very useful to have subscripted variables. Fortunately BASIC has provisions for subscripts that can be applied to either string or numeric variables that are ready and waiting for our use.

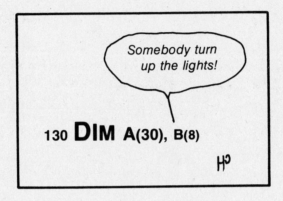

Consider the following set of numeric information:

i	Y_i
1	14
2	8
3	9
4	11
5	16
6	20
7	5
8	3

We can refer to the entire set of numbers with the single name Y. Thus, Y is a "collection of numbers, a matrix, or an array"—all of which mean roughly the same thing for our purposes. To locate a number in the array, we must have the array name (in this case Y) and the position within the array. Here is where the I column is used. Thus Y(3) which is read as "Y sub three" locates the third number in the array Y. In this case, Y(3) has the value 9. Likewise, Y(7) is 5, Y(1) is 14, and so on. Generally we can speak of Y(I), which we read as "Y sub I" and which denotes any element of the array depending on the value of I. If I were 8, then Y(I) would be 3 in our example. This collection of numbers is one-dimensional since only one number (subscript) is needed to locate any element in the array.

Next let's look at a two-dimensional numeric array.

$Y_{i,j}$	1	2	3	4
1	3	−1	10	8
2	2	4	5	6
3	1	−2	9	3

Now we need two numbers to locate an element in the array. Given a row number and a column number, we can find any element of the array we desire. For example, Y(1,3) means the element of Y located at row 1, column 3. In the example above, the element has the value 10. In general, we denote an element in the two-dimensional array as Y(I,J). The first subscript (I) is the row number, and the second subscript (J) is the column number.

To make sure you understand how the double subscripts are used, refer to the two-dimensional array in the table above and verify that the following statements are correct:

$$Y_{3,2} = -2$$
$$Y_{1,4} = 8$$
$$Y_{3,3} = 9$$
$$Y_{2,1} = 2$$

In BASIC, subscripts are enclosed in parentheses following the array name. Thus, Y(2) means "Y sub two" and does not indicate Y multiplied by (2). B$(5,8) means "B$ sub five eight." An interesting question comes up. Does X(M–N,S*T) mean anything? The answer is yes provided that PET can convert M–N and S*T into numbers. Even Y(Y(1,1),Y(2,3)) is all right as long as PET can locate the numbers in Y(1,1) and Y(2,3). However, there is an important point to be remembered. Suppose we want to look up X(A+B) where A = 2.6 and B = 1.1 Thus, A+B = 3.7, but it doesn't make any sense to try to look up the 3.7th number in the array X. Accordingly, the computer will take the integer part of 3.7, and X(A+B) works out to be X(3), the third element in the array X.

Everything that has been said about numeric arrays applies to character-string arrays. By this time you should be familiar enough with the concept that we do not need the word "character" any more. It should be clear that "string array" refers to a collection of characters. So, from this point on we will use the terms "string array" and "string variable" rather than "character-string array" and "character-string variable."

An example of a one-dimensional string array is

```
X$(1) = "SON"
X$(2) = "DAUGHTER"
X$(3) = "MOTHER"
X$(4) = "FATHER"
X$(5) = "UNCLE"
X$(6) = "AUNT"
```

The words comprise the elements of the array. The numbers 1 through 6 are the subscripts that locate a particular word in the array. PET handles subscripts in string arrays in the same manner as it handles numeric arrays.

An example of a two dimensional string array is

```
A$(1,1) = "AA"        A$(1,2) = "AB"
A$(2,1) = "BA"        A$(2,2) = "BB"
A$(3,1) = "CA"        A$(3,2) = "CB"
```

Here the elements are pairs of characters to illustrate that string array elements are just collections of characters. They need not be words.

One final comment about string variables. String variables can be read from DATA statements in the same fashion as numeric variables. If strings are to be used in DATA statements, be safe and enclose them in quotation marks. If a READ statement contains both numeric and string variables, you must be careful that the information in the DATA statements matches the type of information being asked for. If, for example, PET is trying to read a string variable, and the next information in the DATA statements is numeric, the computer will halt and signal an error.

Saving Space for Arrays

PET must know how big an array is for two reasons. First, there is a question of how much space to save in memory to hold the array. Next, the computer must know the size of the array in order to carry out arithmetic operations properly. Actually, for small arrays, BASIC saves space automatically. If a one-dimensional array is used in a program, BASIC automatically sets up space for ten elements if there is no DIM statement. If a two-dimensional array is used, BASIC will save enough space in memory for a ten by ten array if no DIM statement is in the program. It probably isn't wise to use this feature of BASIC. We will emphasize the routine use of DIMension statements in all programs regardless of the size of the arrays. Troubleshooting a program that uses arrays is very difficult if no DIM statement is present.

Save space with a
DIM
statement.

An example of a DIM (for "DIMension") statement is

```
100 DIM B(5,20),Y(8),Z(34),X$(3,6)
```

Four arrays are dimensioned in line 100. B is a two-dimensional numeric array having five rows and twenty columns. Y is a one-dimensional numeric array with eight elements. Likewise, Z is numeric, one-dimensional, and has thirty-four elements. Finally, X$ is a string array with three rows and six columns. It's a good practice to make the DIM statement the first one in the program. This way it is easy to glance at the beginning of the program to see the sizes of the arrays that will be used.

At any rate, the DIM statement must be before any other statements that refer to arrays. As indicated above, it is also a good practice to use a DIM statement in all programs, whether or not BASIC demands it.

Subscripted Variables and FOR NEXT Loops

Since subscripts involve collections of data and operations with collections of data almost always involve repetition, it seems reasonable that we should employ FOR NEXT statements to handle arrays. As an example, the following program segment will set up a six by four array, then load 5s into all the elements.

```
100 DIM A(6,4)
110 FOR R = 1 TO 6
120 FOR C = 1 TO 4
130 A(R,C) = 5
140 NEXT C
150 NEXT R
```

If we trace this program segment, the details of the process become clear. When line 130 in the program is reached the first time, R = 1 and C = 1. Then R is held constant while C goes to 2, 3, and 4. At each step in this process, the corresponding element of the array is set equal to 5. Then R is set equal to 2, and C takes on the values 1, 2, 3, and 4. The process goes on until all the elements of the array have been set equal to 5.

Either one- or two-dimensional arrays can be handled in this fashion using subscripts. Loops and arrays provide a new measure of muscle for the PET and begins to reveal the power it possesses.

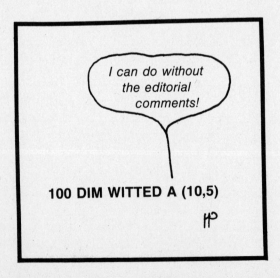

I can do without the editorial comments!

100 DIM WITTED A (10,5)

8-4 PROGRAM EXAMPLES

The use of subscripted variables permits many interesting problems to be handled easily in BASIC. We will look at several programs to illustrate how subscripts are used.

Example 1 - Examination Grades

To illustrate the concept of a one-dimensional array, let's take an example that is near and dear to the hearts of most people—a set of examination grades. Suppose that we have the following results on an examination given to a class of fifteen students.

Student Number

	1	2	3	4	5	6	7	8	9	10	11	12	13	14	15
Grade	67	82	94	75	48	64	89	91	74	71	65	83	72	69	72

The problem is to write a BASIC program to allow the class grades above to be typed in. The format should appear as follows:

```
HOW MANY STUDENTS ? 15
STUDENT          GRADE

1                ? 67
2                ? 82
3                ? 94
4                ? 75
5                ? 48
6                ? 64
7                ? 89
8                ? 91
9                ? 74
10               ? 71
11               ? 65
12               ? 83
13               ? 72
14               ? 69
15               ? 72
```

The program should compute the class average, the highest grade, and the lowest grade, and print this information out as follows:

```
CLASS AVERAGE IS 74.4
HIGHEST GRADE IS 94
LOWEST GRADE IS 48
```

As in past exercises, let's take this by steps. First, since we are going to store the student grades in subscripted form, we must include a DIM statement to save space for the array.

```
100 DIM G(50)
```

We are using the variable G to store grades and can insert up to fifty grades. Next we have a message, an input, and a space.

```
110 PRINT "HOW MANY STUDENTS";
120 INPUT N
130 PRINT
```

Now we are ready to input the grades. First the heading for the table must be generated.

```
140 PRINT "STUDENT","GRADE"
150 PRINT
```

A loop using FOR NEXT statements is ideal to control the input of grades.

```
160 FOR I = 1 TO N
170 PRINT I,
180 INPUT G(I)
190 NEXT I
```

The student number is printed out in line 170. In line 180, the student number (I) is used as a subscript for the grade. This generates grades in the computer in the form G(1), G(2), ..., G(N). The next task is to find the average of the grades. This can be done by summing up all the grades and dividing by the number of grades.

```
200 S = 0
210 FOR I = 1 TO N
220 S = S+G(I)
230 NEXT I
240 PRINT
```

Now we compute the average and print out the results.

```
250 M = S/N
260 PRINT "CLASS AVERAGE IS";M
```

The final part of the program is to locate and print out the highest and lowest grades in the class. H and L will stand for the highest and lowest grades, respectively. Initially we will set both H and L equal to the first grade in the list which is G(1). We know that the same grade can't be the highest and lowest at the same time. Thus, we will go through the rest of the grades, compare H and L with each grade, and make adjustments to H and L as required.

```
270 H = G(1)
280 L = G(1)
290 FOR I = 2 TO N
300 IF L < G(I) THEN 320
310 L = G(I)
320 IF H > G(I) THEN 340
330 H = G(I)
340 NEXT I
```

The required printout can be obtained with two lines.

```
350 PRINT "HIGHEST GRADE IS";H
360 PRINT "LOWEST GRADE IS";L
```

Finally the END statement completes the program.

```
370 END
```

The complete program follows:

```
100 DIM G(50)
110 PRINT "HOW MANY STUDENTS";
120 INPUT N
130 PRINT
140 PRINT "STUDENT","GRADE"
150 PRINT
160 FOR I = 1 TO N
170 PRINT I,
180 INPUT G(I)
190 NEXT I
200 S = 0
210 FOR I = 1 TO N
220 S = S+G(I)
230 NEXT I
240 PRINT
250 M = S/N
260 PRINT "CLASS AVERAGE IS";M
270 H = G(1)
280 L = G(1)
290 FOR I = 2 TO N
300 IF L < G(I) THEN 320
310 L = G(I)
320 IF H > G(I) THEN 340
330 H = G(I)
340 NEXT I
350 PRINT "HIGHEST GRADE IS";H
360 PRINT "LOWEST GRADE IS";L
370 END
```

RUN this program on your PET using the DATA at the beginning of the discussion. If you have any difficulty with the highest and lowest search in lines 270 through 340, trace the program in detail.

Example 2 - Course Grades

We can easily extend the ideas in Example 1 to a two-dimensional array. Now, suppose we have a class with ten students, and the course grade is based upon five examinations. Typical results for such a class might be

Student Number

		1	2	3	4	5	6	7	8	9	10
	1	92	71	81	52	75	97	100	63	41	75
	2	85	63	79	49	71	91	93	58	52	71
Exam	3	89	74	80	61	79	88	97	55	51	73
	4	96	68	84	58	80	93	95	61	47	70
	5	82	72	82	63	73	92	93	68	56	74

We will use FOR NEXT commands to READ the data from DATA statements. The computer is to compute and print out the following information:

```
STUDENT            COURSE AVE.

1                  (Computer prints average, etc.)
2
3
(etc.)


TEST               CLASS AVE.

1                  (Computer prints average, etc.)
2
3
(etc.)
```

The program must start with a DIM statement although the DATA statements can go anywhere in the program.

```
100 DIM G(5,10)
```

This reserves memory space for an array with five rows and ten columns. The row number (R) will be the examination number, and the column number (C) will correspond to the student number.

```
110 DATA 92,71,81,52,75,97,99,63,41,75
120 DATA 85,63,79,49,71,91,93,58,52,71
130 DATA 89,74,80,61,79,88,97,55,51,73
140 DATA 96,68,84,58,80,93,95,61,47,70
150 DATA 82,72,82,63,73,92,93,68,56,74
```

Now we must read the data into the program.

```
160 FOR R = 1 TO 5
170 FOR C = 1 TO 10
180 READ G(R,C)
190 NEXT C
200 NEXT R
```

This causes the numbers to be read into the matrix G by rows. Thus, the data in line 110 become row 1 of the matrix G, the data in line 120 become row 2 of the matrix, and so forth. Before doing anything else, we must print out the required headings.

```
210 PRINT "STUDENT","COURSE AVE."
220 PRINT
```

Now we can compute the course average for each student.

```
230 FOR C = 1 TO 10
```

Line 230 opens a loop that will look at each column in the matrix. For each value of C, we must compute the column average and print it out.

```
240 S = 0
250 FOR R = 1 TO 5
260 S = S+G(R,C)
270 NEXT R
280 PRINT C,S/5
```

Then, the C loop must be closed.

```
290 NEXT C
```

Now the process is repeated except that the averages are computed on rows rather than columns.

```
300 PRINT
310 PRINT "TEST","CLASS AVE."
320 PRINT
330 FOR R = 1 TO 5
340 S = 0
350 FOR C = 1 TO 10
360 S = S+G(R,C)
370 NEXT C
380 PRINT R,S/10
390 NEXT R
```

Finally we have the END statement.

```
400 END
```

The complete program follows:

```
100 DIM G(5,10)
110 DATA 92,71,81,52,75,97,99,63,41,75
120 DATA 85,63,79,49,71,91,93,58,52,71
130 DATA 89,74,80,61,79,88,97,55,51,73
140 DATA 96,68,84,58,80,93,95,61,47,70
150 DATA 82,72,82,63,73,92,93,68,56,74
160 FOR R = 1 TO 5
170 FOR C = 1 TO 10
180 READ G(R,C)
190 NEXT C
200 NEXT R
210 PRINT "STUDENT","COURSE AVE."
220 PRINT
230 FOR C = 1 TO 10
240 S = 0
250 FOR R = 1 TO 5
260 S = S+G(R,C)
270 NEXT R
280 PRINT C,S/5
290 NEXT C
300 PRINT
310 PRINT "TEST","CLASS AVE."
320 PRINT
330 FOR R = 1 TO 5
340 S = 0
350 FOR C = 1 TO 10
360 S = S+G(R,C)
370 NEXT C
380 PRINT R,S/10
390 NEXT R
400 END
```

Example 3 – Alphabetic Sort

As an example of how a string array might be used, let's design a program to call for the input of a list of words, sort the list into alphabetic order, and then print out the sorted list.

First, we will agree that no more than twenty words will be in the list. Of course, this could be any value we desire, but twenty seems like a good number. If we use A\$ to name the string array, we can write the dimension statement.

```
100 DIM A$(20)
```

Next, let's call for the number of words in a specific list. Under the ground rules, this can be anything up to twenty. Then, we must input the words.

```
110 PRINT "HOW MANY WORDS";
120 INPUT N
130 FOR I = 1 TO N
140 INPUT A$(I)
150 NEXT I
```

Now that the list of words is input, it can be sorted. The program segment below does this.

```
160 FOR I = 1 TO N-1
170 IF A$(I+1) >= A$(I) THEN 220
180 B$ = A$(I+1)
190 A$(I+1) = A$(I)
200 A$(I) = B$
210 GOTO 160
220 NEXT I
```

Study this program segment until you see how it works. If the condition in line 170 is true, the two words being compared are in alphabetical order and the comparison shifts up one place in the list. If not, the set of statements in lines 180 through 200 interchanges the two words. Then from line 210, the whole comparison starts again. This process keeps up until the assertion in line 170 is true for the whole list, at which time the list is in alphabetic order.

The sorted list is now output.

```
230 PRINT
240 FOR I = 1 TO N
250 PRINT A$(I)
260 NEXT I
270 END
```

The complete program is

```
100 DIM A$(20)
110 PRINT "HOW MANY WORDS";
120 INPUT N
130 FOR I = 1 TO N
140 INPUT A$(I)
150 NEXT I
160 FOR I = 1 TO N-1
170 IF A$(I+1) >= A$(I) THEN 220
180 B$ = A$(I+1)
190 A$(I+1) = A$(I)
200 A$(I) = B$
210 GOTO 160
220 NEXT I
230 PRINT
240 FOR I = 1 TO N
250 PRINT A$(I)
260 NEXT I
270 END
```

Try this program out with a list of words of your choosing. Verify that the program does sort the list of words that you input into alphabetic order.

Example 4 – A Graphic Display

As a final example, one that incidentally has nothing in particular to do with arrays, simply RUN the following program:

```
100 FOR I = 2 TO 19
110 PRINT TAB(I);"XX";TAB(40-I);"XX"
120 NEXT I
130 GOTO 100
140 END
```

RUN the program and when you get tired of watching the display, press the STOP key.

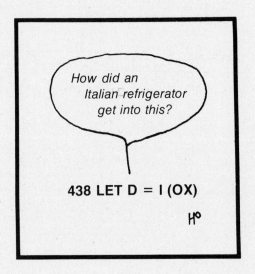

8-5 PROBLEMS

1. Write a program using the DATA statements

```
200 DATA 12
210 DATA 2,1,4,3,2,4,5,6,3,5,4,1
```

which will read the size of an array from the first DATA statement, then read the elements of the array from the second DATA statement, loading them into an array X. Then print out the array.

2. Write a BASIC program to read twenty-five numbers from DATA statements into a one-dimensional array named A. Search the array and print out the number of elements in the array that are greater than fifty. Fill in the required DATA statements with any numbers you choose.

3. What will be output if the following program is RUN?

```
100 DIM Y(6)
110 FOR I = 1 TO 6
120 READ Y(I)
130 NEXT I
140 DATA 2,1,3,1,2,1
150 S1 = 0
160 S2 = 0
170 FOR I = 1 TO 6
180 S1 = S1+Y(I)
190 S2 = S2+Y(I)↑2
200 NEXT I
210 X = S2-S1
220 PRINT X
230 END
```

4. What will be output if the following program is RUN?

```
100 DIM A(10)
110 FOR I = 1 TO 10
120 READ A(I)
130 NEXT I
140 X = A(1)
150 FOR I = 1 TO 9
160 A(I) = A(I+1)
170 NEXT I
180 A(10) = X
190 FOR I = 1 TO 10
200 PRINT A(I)
210 NEXT I
220 DATA 10,9,8,7,6,5,4,3,2,1
230 END
```

5. Write a BASIC program to call for the input of N (assumed to be a whole number between 1 and 100), then input a one-dimensional array with N elements, sort the array into descending order, and finally print out the sorted array. (Hint: Look at the sort in Example 3.)

6. Let's assume that the first number in the DATA statements gives the number of pieces of data to follow. Assume that the pieces of data are all whole numbers between 1 and 10 inclusive. Write a program that will compute the numbers of 1s,

number of 2s, etc., in the data and then print this out. (Hint: Use the data as they are read in as a subscript to increment an element of an array used to count the numbers.)

7. What will be printed out if the following program is RUN?

```
100 DIM Z(6,6)
110 FOR R = 1 TO 6
120 FOR C = 1 TO 6
130 Z(R,C) = 0
140 NEXT C
150 NEXT R
160 FOR R = 1 TO 5 STEP 2
170 FOR C = R TO 6
180 Z(R,C) = 1
190 NEXT C
200 NEXT R
210 FOR R = 1 TO 6
220 FOR C = 1 TO 6
230 PRINT Z(R,C);
240 NEXT C
250 PRINT
260 PRINT
270 NEXT R
280 END
```

8. If the program below is executed, what will the computer print out?

```
100 DIM A(5,5)
110 FOR R = 1 TO 5
120 FOR C = 1 TO 5
130 A(R,C) = 2
140 NEXT C
150 NEXT R
160 FOR C = 5 TO 1 STEP -1
170 FOR R = 1 TO C
180 A(R,C) = 3
190 NEXT R
200 NEXT C
210 FOR R = 1 TO 5
220 FOR C = 1 TO 5
230 PRINT A(R,C);
240 NEXT C
250 PRINT
260 PRINT
270 NEXT R
280 END
```

9. Write a program to read the following array from DATA statements, then print out the array.

$$\begin{bmatrix} 2 & 1 & 0 & 5 & 1 \\ 3 & 2 & 1 & 3 & 1 \end{bmatrix}$$

10. Write a program to read the following array from DATA statements, then print out the array.

$$\begin{bmatrix} 5 & 3 \\ 2 & 0 \\ -1 & 1 \\ 4 & 2 \\ 2 & 6 \end{bmatrix}$$

11. Write a BASIC program that will call for the input of an M by N array. Then compute and print out the sum of the elements in each row and the product of the elements in each column.

12. Write a BASIC program that will read two arrays from DATA statements. Both the arrays are two by three. Then compute another two by three array such that each element is the sum of the corresponding elements in the first two arrays. Print out the third array.

13. The data below represent sales totals made by salespersons over a 1-week period.

		Mon	Tue	Wed	Thu	Fri	Sat
	1	48	40	73	120	100	90
Salesperson	2	75	130	90	140	110	85
	3	50	72	140	125	106	92
	4	108	75	92	152	91	87

Write a program that will compute and print out (a) the daily sales totals, (b) the weekly sales totals for each salesperson, and (c) the total weekly sales.

14. Write a BASIC program to input a list of N names and N grades into two different one-dimensional arrays. Assume that N will not be greater than twenty. Sort the arrays so that the names are in alphabetical order, and the grades are matched correctly with the names. Try out the program on data of your choice.

15. Repeat problem 14 except sort the grades so that they are listed in descending order with the names matched correctly with the grades.

8-6 PRACTICE TEST

Check yourself with the following practice test. The answers are given at the end of the book.

1. What is the purpose of the DIM statement?

_____

2. We have an array named X. What variable name does BASIC use to locate the element in row 3, column 4?

_____

3. What will happen if the following program is RUN?

```
100 DIM A$(4),B(4)
110 FOR I = 1 TO 4
120 READ A$(I),B(I)
130 NEXT I
140 PRINT A$(4),B(2)
150 DATA "HERB",165,"TOM",183
160 DATA "SAM",145,"BILL",192
170 END
```

_____

4. Write a program to input a list of numbers, then find and print out the sum of the positive numbers in the list.

---

5. We have a string array named X. What variable name does BASIC use to locate the element in row 2, column 4?

---

6. Write a program using FOR NEXT statements to load a four by six array with 4s. Then print out the array.

---

7. What will be printed out if the program is RUN?

```
100 DIM A(5,5)
110 FOR I = 1 TO 5
120 FOR J = 1 TO 5
130 A(I,J) = 0
140 NEXT J
150 NEXT I
160 FOR I = 1 TO 5
170 A(I,I) = 2
180 NEXT I
190 FOR I = 1 TO 5
200 FOR J = 1 TO 5
210 PRINT A(I,J);
220 NEXT J
230 PRINT
240 PRINT
250 NEXT J
260 END
```

---

8. The following array is named A:

$$\begin{bmatrix} 1 & 3 & 5 \\ 6 & 2 & 4 \end{bmatrix}$$

a. Write a DIM statement for A.

_____

b. What is the value of A(2,3)?

_____

c. If X = 1 and Y = 2, what is A(X,Y)?

_____

d. What is A(A(1,1),A(2,2))?

_____

"DO-IT-YOURSELF" FUNCTIONS AND SUBROUTINES

9-1 OBJECTIVES

In this chapter we will learn how the PET can be programmed to perform suboperations. This can be done through either program segments or special on-line instructions. Specifically, we will look at the following things.

"Do-It-Yourself" Functions

We have previously seen functions that are built into BASIC. Now we will learn how to define our own functions to carry out any desired task.

Subroutines

When complicated operations are to be repeated, subroutines may be very useful. We will explore how subroutines can be set up and used in BASIC programs.

Program Applications

Sometimes it is difficult for the beginner to see the value of user-defined functions and subroutines. These ideas will be stressed in our continued attention to programming in BASIC.

9-2 DISCOVERY ACTIVITIES

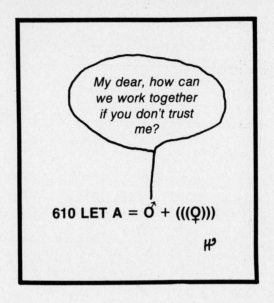

1. Turn your PET on and enter the following program:

```
100 DEF FNA(X) = 5*X+4
110 X = 2
120 Y = 5*X+4
130 PRINT Y,FNA(2)
140 END
```

RUN the program and record the output below.

_____

2. Change line 130 to read

```
130 PRINT Y,FNA(X)
```

Display the program. What do you think will happen if we RUN this program?

_____

RUN the program. What did happen?

_____

3. Change line 110 to read

```
110 X = 5
```

Display the program and study it. Now what will be output if we RUN the program?

_____

See if you were right. RUN the program and record what happened.

_____

4. Now change line 130 to read

```
130 PRINT Y,FNA(5)
```

Display the program. What to you think this program will do?

_____

RUN the program and write down the output.

_____

5. Notice that the expressions after the equal signs in lines 100 and 120 of your program are the same. In one of the versions of the program, we printed out Y and FNA(X) and saw that they were the same. Let's follow up on this information. Clear out the program in memory and enter the following program:

```
100 DEF FNA(X) = X↑2
110 DEF FNB(X) = 3*X
120 DEF FNC(X) = X+2
130 X = 1
140 PRINT FNA(X),FNB(X),FNC(X)
150 END
```

Study the program carefully. What do you think will be printed out if the program is executed?

_____

Now RUN the program and write down what happened.

_____

Substitute 1 for X in the expressions on the right side of lines 100, 110, and 120 in your program. Write down the numbers you obtain.

_____

Now compare these numbers with those typed out by PET.

6. Change line 130 to read

```
130 X = 2
```

Display the program. What will be printed out by the program if it is RUN now?

_____

See if you were right. RUN the program and record the results below.

_____

7. OK, change line 130 to

$$130 \ X \ = \ 3$$

Now what will happen if the program is RUN?

_____

Verify your answer by executing the program and recording what happened.

_____

8. Now on to some more ideas we can explore with this program. Type

```
130 X = 1
140 PRINT FNC(X+4),FNA(X),FNB(2)
```

Display the program. Write down what you think will be printed out if the program is RUN.

_____

RUN the program and record the output.

_____

9. Let's try a slightly different variation on the theme we have been exploring. Type

```
140 PRINT FNA(X),FNB(FNA(X))
```

Display the program and study it carefully. Try to figure out what will be printed out when the program is RUN. Record your answer below.

_____

RUN the program and see if you were correct. Write down below what happened.

_____

10. One last point on this matter. Type

```
130 X = 4
140 PRINT FNA(X),FNC(X),FNA(SQR(X))
```

Now what will happen in the program?

_____

Execute the program and record what happened.

_____

11. Clear out the program in memory. Enter the following program:

```
100 PRINT "A";
110 GOSUB 200
120 PRINT "B";
130 GOSUB 300
140 PRINT "C";
150 STOP
200 PRINT 1;
210 RETURN
300 PRINT 2;
310 RETURN
400 END
```

This program has three new statements that you haven't seen so far. These are GOSUB, RETURN, and STOP. The program itself is intended only to provide practice in tracing these new statements. Execute the program and record the output.

_____

Compare what was printed out with the program lines that caused the printout.

12. The GOSUB statement in line 110 transfers the program to which statement? (Hint: Look at the printout in step 11.)

13. The RETURN statement in line 210 transfers the program to which statement? (Hint: Again, examine the printout in step 11.)

14. The line numbers below indicate the flow of the program as it is executed.

Line Number	What Happens
100	Print out A
110	Transfer to line 200
200	Print out 1
210	Transfer to line 120
120	Print out B

130	Transfer to line 300
300	Print out 2
310	Transfer to line 140
140	Print out C
150	Transfer to line 400
400	End of program

Study this carefully and follow through with the program. Can you see the purpose of the GOSUB and RETURN statements yet? What about the STOP statement?

15. Clear out the program in your work space. Enter the following program:

```
100 REM SUBR. DEMO
110 DIM X(4)
120 READ X(1),X(2),X(3),X(4)
130 REM SORT
140 GOSUB 300
150 REM PRINT
160 GOSUB 400
170 X(3) = 7
180 REM SORT
190 GOSUB 300
200 REM PRINT
210 GOSUB 400
220 STOP
300 REM SORT SUBR
310 FOR I = 1 TO 3
320 IF X(I+1) > X(I) THEN 370
330 C = X(I+1)
340 X(I+1) = X(I)
350 X(I) = C
360 GOTO 310
370 NEXT I
380 RETURN
400 REM PRINT SUBR.
410 PRINT X(1),X(2),X(3),X(4)
420 RETURN
500 DATA 2,1,5,6
600 END
```

Display the program and check that you have entered it correctly. This program furnishes an example of how a subroutine might be used. The subroutine in lines 300 through 380 sorts the array X into ascending order. The subroutine in lines

400 through 420 prints out the array. RUN the program and record the output.

Note that the original array is

$$2 \qquad 1 \qquad 5 \qquad 6$$

You can see this by checking the DATA statement in the program. In line 140, the program jumps to the subroutine and a sort of the numbers is done. After the program returns to line 150, the sorted array is now

$$1 \qquad 2 \qquad 5 \qquad 6$$

In line 170 we change the third element of the array, then branch to the subroutine for another sorting. After the return to line 200, the sorted array

$$1 \qquad 2 \qquad 6 \qquad 7$$

is printed out. Finally, the STOP command in line 200 causes the program to jump to the END statement. Clearly we could sort the array X as often as desired by merely inserting a statement GOSUB 300. This is certainly more efficient than writing out the instructions for sorting each time it is desired.

16. This completes the computer work for this chapter.

9-3 DISCUSSION

Now we need to examine the ideas introduced in the computer work. Once you understand clearly how the computer handles these concepts, you will have powerful new skills to use in your programs.

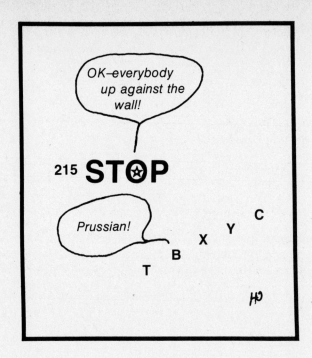

"Do-It-Yourself" Functions

The DEF (an abbreviation for "define") statement permits us to have user-specified functions in BASIC in addition to those functions (SQR, INT, etc.) already built into the language. The form of all DEF statements is the same.

<line #> DEF FN<letter><variable> = <expression using variable>

```
100 DEF FNP(X) = X↑2-3*X
```

Since there are twenty-six letters in the alphabet that could follow FN, we could conceivably have twenty-six defined functions in a single program. The variable (e.g., X in FNP(X)) must appear in the expression on the right side of the equal sign.

If the DEF statement in line 100 were used in a program, and later on the expression FNP(2) were used, the computer would identify that FNP was defined in line 100 and would substitute 2 for X on the right side of the equal sign in the DEF statement, with the result that

$$FNP(2) = -2$$

Likewise, if T = 5, then

$$FNP(T) \ = \ 10$$

The built-in functions in BASIC may be used in the DEF statements. For example,

```
100 DEF FNB(Y) = SQR(Y↑1.5)+3*Y
```

is OK. You can use other defined functions in a DEF statement as illustrated by the following:

```
100 DEF FNB(Y) = FNA(Y)+SQR(Y)
```

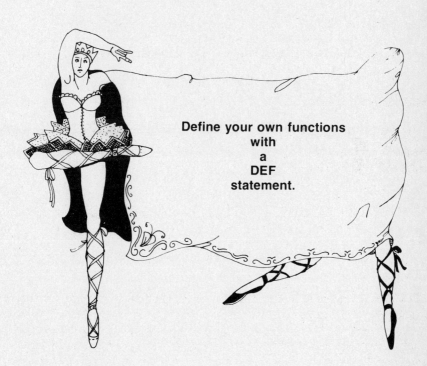

**Define your own functions
with
a
DEF
statement.**

The primary purpose of the user-specified functions that are set up with the DEF statements is to simplify programming by avoiding repeated use of complicated expressions. The wise programmer should be alert for opportunities to save effort with the use of DEF statements.

Subroutines

One of the limitations of the DEF statements is that only a single variable may be involved and we are limited to a single line. More complicated situations in which we want to carry out the same process many times in a program are bound to come up. Here is where subroutines are very useful. The diagram below indicates how a subroutine might be used in a program.

```
Main program begins    ————————————————————
                       ————————————————————
                       ————————————————————
                       200   GOSUB 1000
                       210
                       ————————————————————
                       ————————————————————
                       350   GOSUB 1000
                       360
                       ————————————————————
Main program ends      430   STOP
Subroutine begins      1000   REM SUBROUTINE
                       ————————————————————
                       ————————————————————
End of subroutine      1150   RETURN
End of program         1200   END
```

If the typical program above were executed, when the computer reached the GOSUB in line 200, the program would jump to the beginning of the subroutine in line 1000. The subroutine would be executed, and when the RETURN was encountered in line 1150, control would be passed to the next higher line number after the GOSUB that put us in the subroutine. In this case the program would jump back to line 210. Then the computer would proceed through the main program to the GOSUB in line 350 which would again branch control to the subroutine in line 1000. This time the RETURN would jump back in the program to line 360.

Of course, we could have used GOSUB 1000 as many times as we wanted in the program or could have had as many subroutines as needed. Generally, the top part of the program is the main program and the subroutines are grouped together at the end. There is a good reason for this. We want to perform the subroutines only when called for by a GOSUB. Thus, after the main program is finished, we put a STOP statement in the program. This is precisely the same as a GOTO the END statement and jumps across all the subroutines grouped together at the end of the program. We can use the STOP statement anywhere there is a logical end to the program. This may occur several times in any given program.

**Transfer
to
subroutines
with
GO SUB.**

It is possible, and sometimes desirable, to jump to a subroutine from a subroutine. The diagram below indicates how the computer treats such an event.

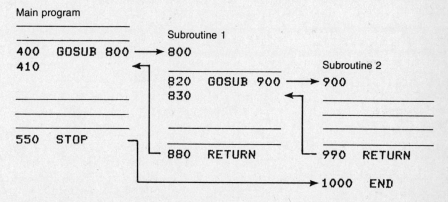

Note that control passes from 400 to 800, on down to 820, to 900, and on down to the RETURN in line 990. Of course, the question here is, does the RETURN take us back to line 410 or line 830? The answer is determined by the rule that the RETURN takes us back to the next statement after the GOSUB that put us in the subroutine containing the RETURN. We are in subroutine 2 because of the GOSUB in line 820; hence the RETURN in line 990 branches us back to line 830. The same rule applies when we reach the RETURN in line 880. At that point we are in subroutine 1 and were put there by the GOSUB in line 400. Thus, the RETURN in line 880 carries us back to line 410. Finally, the STOP statement in line 550 jumps control to the END statement in line 1000.

At this point it may not be clear to you why subroutines are valuable. The need for subroutines becomes more evident as you acquire more skill as a programmer. It is enough at this time to point out that subroutines are extremely important and are considered to be one of the most powerful tools available to the programmer.

9-4 PROGRAM EXAMPLES

Several programs should assist you to master the ideas involved in both user-defined functions and subroutines.

Example 1 - Rounding Off Dollar Values to Cents

Business applications generally involve printing out the results of calculations in dollars and cents. Since PET handles nine significant figures in calculations, we might get an amount like 23.1597643 typed out. This looks strange, and to solve the problem, we should round off the figure to the nearest cent, or 23.16.

This is an ideal application of a user-defined function. Let's write a program that will produce the following typical output when RUN:

```
LABEL PRICE ? 22.80
10% DISCOUNT IS 20.52
15% DISCOUNT IS 19.38
20% DISCOUNT IS 18.24
```

All dollar values typed out should be rounded off to the nearest cent.

First, we must define a function to do the rounding. Such a function is

```
100 DEF FNR(X) = INT(X*100+.5)/100
```

To see how this rule works, suppose X = 23.1597643. We can follow this value through the expression to see what happens.

$$X^*100 = 2315.97$$
$$X^*100+0.5 = 2316.47$$
$$INT\ (X^*100+0.5) = 2316$$
$$INT(X^*100+0.5)/100 = 23.16$$

Therefore 23.1597643 was correctly rounded up to 23.16.

As a second example, suppose that X = 23.1454725. Then

$$X*100 = 2315.47$$
$$X*100+0.5 = 2315.97$$
$$INT(X*100+0.5) = 2315$$
$$INT(X*100+0.5)/100 = 23.15$$

with the result that 23.1547256 was correctly rounded down to 23.15.
The next few lines of the program are self-explanatory.

```
110 PRINT "LABEL PRICE";
120 INPUT Z
130 PRINT "10% DISCOUNT IS";FNR(.9*Z)
140 PRINT "15% DISCOUNT IS";FNR(.85*Z)
150 PRINT "20% DISCOUNT IS";FNR(.8*Z)
```

If desired, we can loop back to the beginning with

```
160 GOTO 110
```

and then end the program.

```
170 END
```

The complete program is

```
100 DEF FNR(X) = INT(X*100+.5)/100
110 PRINT "LABEL PRICE";
120 INPUT Z
130 PRINT "10% DISCOUNT IS";FNR(.9*Z)
140 PRINT "15% DISCOUNT IS";FNR(.85*Z)
150 PRINT "20% DISCOUNT IS";FNR(.8*Z)
160 GOTO 110
170 END
```

In lines 130, 140, and 150 the defined function is used. For a 10 percent discount, the selling price is 90 percent of the original label price Z. Hence we print out FNR(0.9*Z), which rounds off the value to the nearest cent as desired. Note the economy of using the defined function rather than writing out the expression in line 100 each time we want to print out a rounded dollar amount.

Example 2 – Carpet Estimating

We want to write a program that uses a subroutine to compute the price of installed carpet. Suppose that there are four grades of carpet and each is discounted as the quantity of carpet ordered increases. We will assume that the price structure is as follows:

		Price per square yard		
		1	**2**	**3**
	A	$10.00	$ 8.50	$ 7.25
Grade	**B**	13.25	12.00	9.75
	C	16.00	14.00	11.25
	D	20.00	17.20	15.25

1: First 15 square yards

2: Any part of the order exceeding 15 but not more than 25 square yards

3: Anything over 25 square yards

When RUN, the program should produce the following typical output:

```
HOW MANY ROOMS ? 4
FOR EACH ROOM TYPE IN
LENGTH AND WIDTH IN FEET
SEPARATED BY A COMMA


ROOM      DIMENSIONS

1           ? 10,12
2           ? 12,15
3           ? 12,8
4           ? 15,25
85.67 SQ YDS REQUIRED

CARPET GRADE      ORDER COST

A                 674.83
B                 910.25
C                 1062.5
D                 1197.17
```

Before getting involved in the program, we should think a bit about the output. Since the output is in dollars and cents, we may as well use the defined function from Example 1 to take care of rounding off the answers properly. We can also use the rounding function to round off the number of yards of carpet required to the nearest hundredth. So let's begin the program with that defined function.

```
100 DEF FNR(X) = INT(X*100+.5)/100
```

The next few lines follow without difficulty.

```
110 PRINT "HOW MANY ROOMS";
120 INPUT N
130 PRINT "FOR EACH ROOM, TYPE IN"
140 PRINT "LENGTH AND WIDTH IN FEET"
150 PRINT "SEPARATED BY A COMMA"
160 PRINT
170 PRINT "ROOM","DIMENSION"
180 PRINT
```

Now we are ready to call for the input of the room dimensions. We will use the variable A to keep track of the area of the rooms. Remember that the area of a room is its length times its width.

```
190 A = 0
200 FOR I = 1 TO N
210 PRINT I,
220 INPUT L,W
230 A = A+L*W
240 NEXT I
```

Since the total room area is now in square feet, we must divide this by 9 to convert to square yards, and then we will print out the quantity of carpet required.

```
250 A = A/9
260 PRINT FNR(A);"SQ YARDS REQUIRED"
```

At this point we may as well include the price table in the program in the form of DATA statements.

```
270 DATA 10,8.5,7.25
280 DATA 13.25,12,9.75
290 DATA 16,14,11.25
300 DATA 20,17.2,15.25
```

Next we can print out the heading required for the price printout.

```
310 PRINT
320 PRINT "CARPET GRADE","ORDER COST"
330 PRINT
```

Now we come to the point in the program where the subroutine will be useful. Since we don't know precisely where the subroutine should begin, we will simply use a large line number and correct it later if needed.

```
340 REM COMPUTE PRICE FOR GRADE A
350 GOSUB 800
```

Let's write the subroutine now. First, for each of the grades of carpet we need the three prices. We can do this by reading them from the DATA statements.

```
800 REM SUBROUTINE TO COMPUTE CARPET PRICE
810 READ C1,C2,C3
```

Next we check to see if the area of the carpet is less than 15, between 15 and 25, or more than 25 square yards and then compute the price accordingly.

```
820 IF A > 25 THEN 860
830 IF A > 15 THEN 880
840 P = C1*A
850 GOTO 890
860 P = 15*C1+10*C2+(A-25)*C3
870 GOTO 890
880 P = 15*C1+(A-15)*C2
890 RETURN
```

Trace this program segment through to convince yourself that the price is being computed correctly. Now we can return to the main program and print out the first price.

```
360 PRINT "A",,,FNR(P)
```

Once this pattern has been established, the rest of the main program follows easily.

```
370 REM COMPUTE PRICE FOR GRADE B
380 GOSUB 800
390 PRINT "B",,,FNR(P)
400 REM COMPUTE PRICE FOR GRADE C
410 GOSUB 800
420 PRINT "C",,,FNR(P)
430 REM COMPUTE PRICE FOR GRADE D
440 GOSUB 800
450 PRINT "D",,,FNR(P)
460 STOP
```

The STOP statement in line 460 is needed to prevent the program from falling into the subroutine. The value of the subroutine becomes clear when we see that had it not been available, each of the four GOSUB statements would have had to be replaced with as many statements as in the subroutine.

The complete program is

```
100 DEF FNR(X) = INT(X*100+.5)/100
110 PRINT "HOW MANY ROOMS";
120 INPUT N
130 PRINT "FOR EACH ROOM, TYPE IN"
140 PRINT "LENGTH AND WIDTH IN FEET"
150 PRINT "SEPARATED BY A COMMA"
160 PRINT
170 PRINT "ROOM","DIMENSIONS"
180 PRINT
190 A = 0
200 FOR I = 1 TO N
210 PRINT I,
220 INPUT L,W
230 A = A+L*W
240 NEXT I
250 A = A/9
260 PRINT FNR(A);"SQ YARDS REQUIRED"
270 DATA 10,8.5,7.25
280 DATA 13.25,12,9.75
290 DATA 16,14,11.25
300 DATA 20,17.2,15.25
310 PRINT
```

```
320 PRINT "CARPET GRADE","ORDER COST"
330 PRINT
340 REM COMPUTE PRICE FOR GRADE A
350 GOSUB 800
360 PRINT "A",,FNR(P)
370 REM COMPUTE PRICE FOR GRADE B
380 GOSUB 800
390 PRINT "B",,FNR(P)
400 REM COMPUTE PRICE FOR GRADE C
410 GOSUB 800
420 PRINT "C",,FNR(P)
430 REM COMPUTE PRICE FOR GRADE D
440 GOSUB 800
450 PRINT "D",,FNR(P)
460 STOP
800 REM SUBROUTINE TO COMPUTE CARPET PRICE
810 READ C1,C2,C3
820 IF A > 25 THEN 860
830 IF A > 15 THEN 880
840 P = C1*A
850 GOTO 890
860 P = 15*C1+10*C2+(A-25)*C3
870 GOTO 890
880 P = 15*C1+(A-15)*C2
890 RETURN
900 END
```

Example 3 - Screen Graphics

We have not yet used the fact that the cursor can be moved around the screen under program control. Our problem will be to write subroutines to position the cursor on the screen and then draw bold lines under program control.

Before getting into the program we should note that there are twenty-five rows and forty columns on the screen where characters can be printed. Thus, by specifying a row number between 1 and 25 and a column number between 1 and 40, we can reach any position on the screen.

First let's write a subroutine that will move the cursor from the "home" (or upper left corner) position to row R, column C. Such a subroutine follows:

```
400 REM POSITION CURSOR AT R,C
410 FOR I = 1 TO R
420 PRINT "Q";
430 NEXT I
440 FOR J = 1 TO C
450 PRINT "]";
460 NEXT J
470 RETURN
```

This subroutine moves the cursor down R rows from the home position. The graphic character in the PRINT statement in line 420 is the PET representation of the "cursor down" arrow. Then the subroutine moves the cursor C colums to the right. The graphic symbol between quotes in line 450 is the PET representation of the "cursor right" arrow. When this subroutine is called, then the cursor will be moved R rows down and L rows to the right. To work correctly the cursor should be in the home position before the subroutine is called.

Next we want to be able to draw a horizontal line L characters long beginning at the cursor position. This is done with

```
500 REM DRAW HORIZ LINE (L)
510 FOR K = 1 TO L
520 PRINT "█";
530 NEXT K
540 PRINT "S"
550 RETURN
```

This subroutine follows without particular difficulty. The graphic character in line 520 is the one that will be used to form the line. The graphic character in line 540 is the PET representation of "HOME" which returns the cursor to the upper left corner of the screen.

Finally we need a subroutine to draw a vertical line L characters long beginning at the cursor position. Such a subroutine is

```
600 REM DRAW VERT LINE (L)
610 FOR K = 1 TO L
620 PRINT "█";
630 PRINT "TQ"
640 NEXT K
650 PRINT "S"
660 RETURN
```

This subroutine functions the same as the previous one. The only difference is in line 630. Since we are drawing vertical lines from the top down, each time a character is printed, the cursor must be moved left one space and down one space. The graphic characters in quotes in line 630 are the PET representation of the "cursor left" and "cursor down" arrows.

Now that we have the subroutines available we can write a program to draw a set of lines on the screen. Our problem will be to set up the screen for a Tic-Tac-Toe game. Two vertical lines will be drawn from R = 6, C = 1, and R = 6, C = 17, each seventeen characters long. Then, two horizontal lines eighteen characters long will be drawn from R = 11, C = 6, and R = 11, C = 6. The program is

```
100 REM SET UP FOR TIC TAC TOE
110 REM CLEAR SCREEN
120 PRINT "♥"
130 L = 17
140 R = 6
150 C = 11
160 GOSUB 400
170 GOSUB 600;
180 C = 17
190 GOSUB 400
200 GOSUB 600
210 C = 6
220 R = 11
230 L = 18
240 GOSUB 400
250 GOSUB 500
260 R = 17
270 GOSUB 400
280 GOSUB 500
290 STOP
```

```
400 REM POSITION CURSOR AT R,C
410 FOR I = 1 TO R
420 PRINT "Q";
430 NEXT I
440 FOR J = 1 TO C
450 PRINT "]";
460 NEXT J
470 RETURN
```

```
500 REM DRAW HORIZ LINE (L)
510 FOR K = 1 TO L
520 PRINT "█";
530 NEXT K
540 PRINT "S"
550 RETURN
```

```
600 REM DRAW VERT LINE (L)
610 FOR K = 1 TO L
620 PRINT "█";
630 PRINT "Q"
640 NEXT K
650 PRINT "S"
660 RETURN
```

The graphic character in line 120 is the PET representation of "clear screen and home." Subroutine 400 positions the cursor. Subroutine 500 draws horizontal lines, and subroutine 600 draws vertical lines.

RUN the program to make sure it works as advertised. You might want to experiment with the subroutines to draw systems of horizontal and vertical lines of your choice.

```
100 LET X = 10
110 GOSUB 130
120 STOP
130 RETURN
140 END
```

9-5 PROBLEMS

1. Trace the program below and write down what will be printed out if the program is executed.

```
100 DEF FNA(X) = 2+X
110 DEF FNB(Y) = 10*Y
120 DEF FNC(Z) = Z↑2
130 R = 2
140 S = 3
150 T = 5
160 PRINT FNC(T),FNA(S),FNB(R)
170 R = S+T
180 PRINT FNA(R)+FNB(S)+FNC(T)
190 END
```

2. What will be printed out if the program below is executed?

```
100 DEF FNX(A) = 6*A
110 DEF FNY(B) = B+10
120 DEF FNZ(C) = C↑3
130 READ P,Q,R
140 DATA 1,2,3
150 PRINT FNX(R),FNZ(P),FNY(Q)
160 PRINT FNY(P+Q)+FNX(R)
170 END
```

3. What will be output by the following program if it is executed?

```
100 DIM A(5)
110 READ A(1),A(2),A(3),A(4),A(5)
120 DATA 6,2,7,1,3
130 GOSUB 500
140 PRINT A(1);A(2);A(3);A(4);A(5)
150 A(3) = 10
160 GOSUB 500
170 PRINT A(1);A(2);A(3);A(4);A(5)
180 A(5) = 8
190 GOSUB 500
200 PRINT A(1);A(2);A(3);A(4);A(5)
210 STOP
500 FOR I = 1 TO 4
510 A(I) = A(I+1)
520 NEXT I
530 RETURN
600 END
```

4. What will be printed out if the program below is executed?

```
100 X = 10
110 GOSUB 500
120 PRINT S
130 X = X/2
140 GOSUB 500
150 PRINT S
160 X = X+3
170 GOSUB 500
180 PRINT S
190 STOP
```

```
500 S = 0
510 FOR Y = 1 TO X
520 S = S+Y
530 NEXT Y
540 RETURN
600 END
```

5. Assume that a one-dimensional array Z contains the numbers to be added together. The first element of the array, Z(1), gives the number of elements that follow in the array and are to be summed. Write a subroutine beginning in line 800 to compute the sum of the elements after Z(1). Assign the sum to the variable T. Terminate the subroutine with a RETURN statement. Assume that the array Z has been properly dimensioned and that the values in the array have been loaded in the main program.

6. X is a one-dimensional array. The first element of the array, X(1), gives the number of pieces of data that follow in the array. Write a subroutine beginning in line 500 to search through the array for the largest value. Assign this value to the variable L. Terminate the subroutine with a RETURN statement. Assume that the array X has been properly dimensioned and loaded with numbers elsewhere.

7. Suppose that as part of a printout we need a series of 45 hearts drawn in a horizontal line across the PET screen. Write a subroutine beginning in line 1000 to do this. Terminate the subroutine with a RETURN statement.

8. Assume that a one-dimensional array Y is loaded with numbers. The first element Y(1) gives the number of elements to follow. We want a subroutine to calculate the mean (M) and the standard deviation (S) of the numbers in the array which follow the first element. Begin the subroutine in line 900 and terminate with a RETURN statement. The formulas for calculation of the mean and standard deviation are given below.

$$\text{Mean} = \text{Sum of values} / N$$

$$\text{Standard deviation} = \sqrt{\frac{N \times (\text{sum of squares of values}) - (\text{sum of values})^2}{N \times (N-1)}}$$

9-6 PRACTICE TEST

Check your progress with the following practice test. The answers are given at the end of the book.

1.If DEF FNA(X) = SQR(X)+3*X, Z = 2.5, and W = 10, what is

  a. FNA(1)

_____

  b. FNA(4)

_____

  c. FNA(9)

_____

  d. FNA(Z*W)

_____

2. What will be printed out if we execute the following program?

```
100 DEF FNR(X) = X*X
110 DEF FNS(X) = 3*X
120 DEF FNT(Y) = Y+1
130 A = 1
140 PRINT FNT(A),FNR(A),FNS(A)
150 M = 4
160 PRINT FNR(SQR(M))
170 END
```

3. With regard to subroutines

  a. How do you pass control from the main program to the subroutine?

_____

b. How do you pass control from the subroutine back to the main program?

_____

c. What is the purpose of the STOP statement?

_____

4. What will be printed out if we RUN the following program?

_____

```
100 A = 1
110 GOSUB 200
120 A = A+4
130 GOSUB 200
140 A = A-2
150 GOSUB 200
160 STOP
200 REM SUBROUTINE
210 IF A < 2 THEN 250
220 IF A = 3 THEN 270
230 PRINT "RED"
240 GOTO 280
250 PRINT "WHITE"
260 GOTO 280
270 PRINT "BLUE"
280 RETURN
900 END
```

TEN

RANDOM NUMBERS AND SIMULATIONS

10-1 OBJECTIVES

One of the most interesting applications of computers concerns simulation of events or processes that involve an element of chance. Examples might be using the computer to simulate gambling games or perhaps investigating the number of bank tellers required to ensure that arriving customers do not have to wait more than a few minutes to be served. In this chapter we will see how the computer can be used to handle problems of this type. Our objectives are as follows.

Characteristics of Random-Number Generators

Computers have a random-number generator function that is the heart of all programs involving the element of chance, or randomness. We will learn how these random-number generators can be employed in BASIC programs.

Random Numbers with Special Characteristics

Generally, the random-number generator is used to produce sets of random numbers with characteristics specified by the programmer. We will see how this is done and how any desired set of numbers can be generated.

Programming and Simulations

The programming exercises and problems in this chapter will involve simulations and applications that involve the element of chance.

10-2 DISCOVERY ACTIVITIES

Setting Up the Random-Number Generator

Before beginning the computer work, we must discuss some important characteristics of random-number generators. By their very nature, these generators produce sequences of numbers that appear to have no pattern or relationship. For a random-number generator to be useful, each time we execute a program that utilizes it we should get a different sequence of numbers. However, this gives rise to an interesting question. Suppose a program that uses random numbers is not working correctly. If the problem is connected with the random numbers, it might be extremely difficult to correct since different random numbers are generated each time the program is executed. Consequently, provisions are always included so that a sequence of random numbers can be repeated each time the program is executed. Remember, that this feature of BASIC should be used only when you are troubleshooting a program.

On the PET we control the type of random-number sequence by the argument of the RND function that generates the numbers. If the argument is positive, a different sequence of numbers is generated each time the program is RUN. If the argument is zero, the same sequence of random numbers is generated.

Now, let's go on to the computer work.

1. Turn your PET on. Unless otherwise specified, we will use a positive argument of the RND function to generate different sequences of random numbers.

2. Enter the following program:

```
100 FOR I = 1 TO 10
110 PRINT RND(1)
120 NEXT I
130 END
```

RUN the program and record the largest and smallest numbers that were printed out.

_____

3. RUN the program again. Did the same numbers appear?

_____

What was the largest number typed out?

_____

What was the smallest number?

_____

4. Clear out the program in memory and enter the following program:

```
100 L = .5
110 S = .5
120 FOR I = 1 TO 100
130 X = RND(1)
140 IF X > L THEN 170
150 IF X < S THEN 190
160 GOTO 200
```

```
170 L = X
180 GOTO 200
190 S = X
200 NEXT I
210 PRINT "LARGEST = ";L
220 PRINT "SMALLEST = ";S
230 END
```

This program examines all the numbers generated by the RND function and keeps track of the largest and smallest numbers generated. As the program stands, it will generate 100 random numbers. RUN the program and record what was typed out.

_____

5. Change line 120 to read

```
120 FOR I = 1 TO 1000
```

Now the program will generate 1000 random numbers. RUN the program and record what was printed out.

_____

Based upon what you have seen thus far, what do you believe is the largest number that will be generated by the RND function?

_____

What about the smallest?

_____

6. Now let's go on to some other ideas associated with random numbers. Clear out the program in memory and enter the following program:

```
100 FOR I = 1 TO 10
110 PRINT INT(2*RND(1))
120 NEXT I
130 END
```

Execute the program and record the output.

_____

What were the only two numbers in the printout?

_____

7. Change line 110 to read as follows:

```
110 PRINT INT(3*RND(1))
```

Display the program. If this program is executed, what numbers do you think will be typed out?

_____

RUN the program and write down the output. Can you predict anything about the sequence or pattern in which the numbers will be typed out?

_____

8. Now change line 110 to read

```
110 PRINT INT(2*RND(1)+1)
```

What do you think the program will do now?

_____

Execute the program and record the output.

_____

9. Modify line 110 as follows:

```
110 PRINT INT(4*RND(1)+4)
```

If the program is executed, what do you think will be printed out?

_____

RUN the program and describe the output.

_____

Any pattern to the output?

_____

10. OK, change line 110 as follows:

```
110 PRINT INT(30*RND(1))/10
```

Display the program and study it carefully. What do you think this program will print out?

_____

Execute the program and describe the printout.

_____

11. Finally, change line 110 to read

```
110 PRINT INT(200*RND(1))/100
```

Display the program in your work space. What do you think will happen if this program is executed?

_____

See if you were right. Execute the program and record the output below.

_____

12. Turn your PET off. This terminates the computer work for now.

10-3 DISCUSSION

Now that you have seen some of the characteristics of the random-number generator on the computer, we can profitably proceed to a complete discussion of the matter.

Random-Number Generators

We will not become involved with the details of how random numbers are generated. It is enough to say that there are several mathematical methods to produce these numbers. The random-number generator is called on with the RND function. This function is used like the other built-in functions in BASIC that were studied previously, but differs in two important respects. Recall that the argument of a function (what the function works on) determines the result. Thus SQR(4) is 2, INT(3.456) is 3, and so forth. However, the argument of the RND function has no effect on the numbers produced. This statement isn't completely true but is close enough to the truth for the point that needs to be made. If you use RND(1) or RND(3) or RND(238) in a program, all will have precisely the same effect. As a matter of fact, a variable can be used as the argument of the RND function. RND(Z) is all right provided that Z has been defined somewhere else in the program. You must be careful about this though, since if Z has not been defined, PET will assign it the value zero. The result is that the random-number function becomes RND(0). This does have an effect as will be discussed.

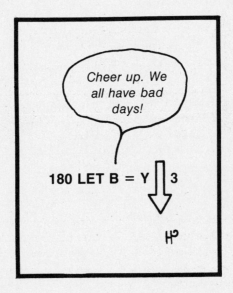

Recall that in the introductory material, it was pointed out that depending on the sign of the argument of the RND function, we can get three different types of sequences. This bears repeating here. First, if the argument is positive, we will get a different sequence of random numbers each time the program is run. If the argument is zero, we will get the same sequence of numbers each time the program is used. Finally, if the argument is negative, we get the same number each time the function is called. So this is the first major difference in the RND function as compared with the others we have studied. The argument has no effect on the function and consequently is known as a "dummy argument." A good rule of thumb is to use 1 as the argument of the RND function.

The second major difference is that there seems to be no pattern or rule used in generating numbers with the RND function. Of course, this is precisely the point of the function. RND stands for "random." The function generates numbers between 0 and 1 at random. All the numbers in the inverval have an equal chance of showing up. Actually, the range of numbers generated is from 0.000000000 to 0.999999999. Zero can show up very rarely, but the number 1 never occurs.

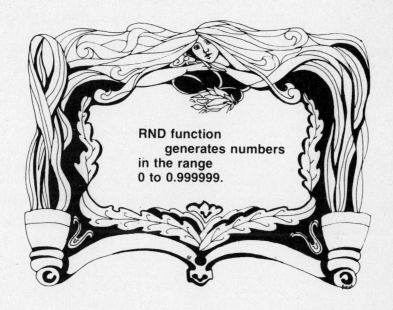

RND function generates numbers in the range 0 to 0.999999.

A good way to visualize how the random-number generator works is to imagine the following situation. We have 1 billion chips numbered 0.000000000, 0.000000001, 0.000000002, and so on up to 0.999999998, and 0.999999999. The chips are all placed in a large container and mixed thoroughly. If we want a random number, we reach into the container and withdraw a single chip, read the number, return the chip to the container, and then mix all the chips again very thoroughly. The RND function works exactly the same way and can be used in BASIC programs anytime we want a random number.

Designing Sets of Random Numbers

Most often we do not want random numbers in the range produced by the RND function, that is, from zero to one. We might want random integers (whole numbers) over a certain range or a set of random numbers with a particular set of characteristics. Therefore, we must give some thought to how to generate sets of random numbers with characteristics we can specify.

Let's begin with the characteristics of random numbers. RND(1) delivers numbers from 0 to just less than one. If we multiply RND(1) by N, we multiply the range of the function by N. Thus N*RND(1) will produce random numbers from zero to just less than N. If desired, we could shift the numbers (keeping the same range) by adding a number. N*RND(0)+A would produce random numbers from A to just less than (A+N). Finally, if desired, we could take the integer part of an expression, using the INT function, to produce random integers. The examples below indicate how the RND function might be used.

BASIC Expression	Result
5*RND(0) + 10	Random numbers in the range 10 to 15
INT(5*RND(0)+10)	Random integers 10,11,12,13,14
INT(2*RND(0)+1)	Random integers 1,2
100*RND(0)	Random numbers in the range 0 to 100

You may have encountered the notion of mean and standard deviation (see problem 8 in Chapter 9). We can use the RND function to generate numbers that appear to be drawn from a collection of numbers having a given mean and standard deviation. The rule for generating these numbers is

$$X = M + S((\text{sum of 12 numbers from RND function}) - 6)$$

where M and S are the desired mean and standard deviation, respectively. This is an application in which a subroutine would be very useful. As defined above, the values of X will appear to be coming from a collection of numbers with mean M and standard deviation S. The values of X can be used to simulate a process following the "bell curve" that is often referred to.

Troubleshooting Programs That Use Random Numbers

We have already pointed out that BASIC provides a way to execute a program several times and repeat the sequence of numbers that are generated by the RND function. It is usually wise to write programs initially so that they do generate the same sequence of numbers each time they are executed. Once you are sure that the program is working correctly, you can modify the program to produce the randomness that is the central idea in the RND function.

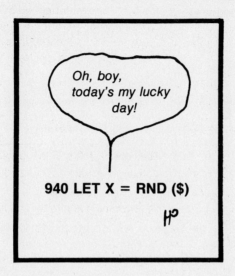

10-4 PROGRAM EXAMPLES

Now we will go through several examples to illustrate how random numbers can be used. Study these examples carefully and make sure you understand exactly what is taking place.

Example 1 - Flipping Coins

One of the easiest applications of random numbers is a coin-tossing simulation. We want to write a program that when executed will produce the following typical printout:

```
TOSS       OUTCOME

1          H
2          T
3          T
4          H
    etc.
```

The outcome is to be determined randomly for each toss of the coin, with both heads and tails having equal probability. The program should print out the results of ten coin tosses.

The first part of the program generates the heading and the space indicated in the printout above.

```
100 PRINT "TOSS","OUTCOME"
110 PRINT
```

Now we must open the loop to generate the ten tosses of the coin.

```
120 FOR I = 1 TO 10
```

The next step is to generate 0s and 1s randomly. We will assume that the occurrence of a 0 means a "head" and the occurrence of a 1 means a "tail." You should be able to convince yourself that the following statement will produce 0s and 1s randomly.

```
130 X = INT(2*RND(1))
```

Now we analyze X to see whether a head (0) or a tail (1) has occurred.

```
140 IF X = 0 THEN 170
150 PRINT I,"T"
160 GOTO 180
170 PRINT I,"H"
180 NEXT I
```

All that remains now is the END statement.

```
190 END
```

The complete program is listed below.

```
100 PRINT "TOSS","OUTCOME"
110 PRINT
120 FOR I = 1 TO 10
130 X = INT(2*RND(1))
140 IF X = 0 THEN 170
150 PRINT I,"T"
160 GOTO 180
170 PRINT I,"H"
180 NEXT I
190 END
```

This is a good program for demonstrating how the computer can be instructed to produce either different sequences of random numbers or identical sequences each time the program is executed. Make the necessary changes in the RND function to see this work.

Example 2 – Random Integers

The next problem is to write a BASIC program to generate and print out fifty random integers (whole numbers) over the range 10 to 15. The only part of the program that will require much thought is the statement to generate the random integers, so we will concentrate on this one statement.

Remember that the RND function generates numbers over the range from zero to slightly less than one. By using the integer function we can convert from random numbers to random integers. INT(6*RND(1)) will produce the integers 0, 1, 2, 3, 4, 5 randomly. Now it is clear that to get the desired numbers, we must add 10. Thus, the expression INT(6*RND(0))+10 will produce the numbers we want.

Once we have this one line figured out, the program follows easily.

```
100 FOR I = 1 TO 50
110 Y = INT(6*RND(1))+10
120 PRINT Y,
130 NEXT I
140 END
```

Example 3 – Birthday Pairs in a Crowd

Suppose that fifty strangers get together in a room. What is the probability that two of the people have the same birthday? We consider only the day of the year, not the year of birth. This problem is a famous one in probability theory and has surprising results. We can attack the problem with the following strategy. By generating random integers over the range 1 to 365, we can simulate a birthday for each of the strangers. If we use a one-dimensional array for the birthdays as they are generated, it is easy to check for identical birthdays. Beginning with the first birthday, B(1), we check to see if it matches any of the remaining ones. Then we do the same thing for B(2), and so on.

For this example, we will depart from the usual method and will look at the complete program, then go back and explain what is taking place in each line.

```
100 DIM B(50)
110 FOR I = 1 TO 50
120 B(I) = INT(365*RND(1))+1
130 NEXT I
140 F = 0
150 FOR I = 1 TO 49
160 FOR J = I+1 TO 50
170 IF B(I) <> THEN 190
180 F = F+1
190 NEXT J
200 NEXT I
210 PRINT "NUMBER OF BIRTHDAY"
220 PRINT "PAIRS FOUND IS"#F
230 END
```

Of course, line 100 merely dimensions an array for fifty elements. Lines 110 through 130 load the array with random integers selected over the range 1 to 365 inclusive. In line 140, we set the variable F equal to zero. We will use this variable to keep track of the number of birthday pairs we find. Line 150 opens a loop to identify the birthday that will be compared with the rest in the list. Since we have to have at least one birthday left in the list to compare with, the value of I stops at 49. In line 160, the second half of the comparison is set up. J begins at the next value past the current value of I and runs through the rest of the list. The test for a birthday pair is made in line 170. If no match is found, we jump to the next value of J. If a match is found, the pair counter is increased by 1 in line 180. The results are printed out in line 210. One problem with the program is that it would record three people having the same birthday as two birthday pairs. Can you figure out a way to fix this?

This is an extremely interesting program to experiment with. The number of people in the crowd can be modified with simple changes in the program. The program can be executed many times to see how many birthday pairs on the average will be found in a crowd of a specified size.

Example 4 – Word Generator

We can use the random-number generator to make up words. Suppose you are given the job to come up with new names for laundry products. You decide that the names should be five characters long. The first, third, and fifth characters will be consonants. The second and fourth characters will be vowels. Random numbers will be used to pick the vowels from the list "AEIOU", and the consonants from the list "BCDFGHJKLMNPQRSTVWXYZ."

We will write a BASIC program to enable the PET to generate a block of twenty words as described above. First we define the string variables that contain the vowels and consonants.

```
100 A$ = "AEIOU"
110 B$ = "BCDFGHJKLMNPQRSTVWXYZ"
```

We will need random integers (whole numbers) over the range 1-5 to select a vowel, and integers over the range 1-21 to select a consonant. This is an ideal application for DEF statements. We will use X as the argument of the DEF statements, and since we want different sets of random numbers each time the program is RUN, will set X equal to 1.

```
120 X = 1
130 DEF FNV(X) = INT(5*RND(X)+1)
140 DEF FNC(X) = INT(21*RND(X)+1)
```

Now we open the loop to generate the words.

```
150 FOR I = 1 TO 20
```

We can use the DEF functions to generate integers, which can in turn be used in the MID$ function to pick out the desired letters from the strings A$ and B$.

```
160 C$ = MID$(B$,FNC(X),1)
170 C$ = C$+MID$(A$,FNV(X),1)
180 C$ = C$+MID$(B$,FNC(X),1)
190 C$ = C$+MID$(A$,FNV(X),1)
200 C$ = C$+MID$(B$,FNC(X),1)
```

In line 160 the first consonant is generated. A vowel, a consonant, and a vowel are added in lines 170, 180, and 190. Finally the last consonant is appended in line 200. The balance of the program follows without difficulty.

```
210 PRINT C$,
220 NEXT I
230 END
```

The complete program follows.

```
100 A$ = "AEIOU"
110 B$ = "BCDFGHJKLMNPQRSTVWXYZ"
120 X = 1
130 DEF FNV(X) = INT(5*RND(X)+1)
140 DEF FNC(X) = INT(21*RND(X)+1)
150 FOR I = 1 TO 20
160 C$ = MID$(B$,FNC(X),1)
170 C$ = C$+MID$(A$,FNV(X),1)
180 C$ = C$+MID$(B$,FNC(X),1)
190 C$ = C$+MID$(A$,FNV(X),1)
200 C$ = C$+MID$(B$,FNC(X),1)
210 PRINT C$,
220 NEXT I
230 END
```

RUN the program a few times and see if your favorite brand names turn up!

Example 5 – Random Graphic Design

As a final example we will see how all the characters available on the keyboard can be displayed radomly on the screen. We will use the subroutine developed in Example 3 in Chapter 9 to position the cursor.

First we want random row numbers (1 to 25), and random column numbers (1 to 40).

```
100 X = 1
110 DEF FNA(X) = INT(25*RND(X)+1)
120 DEF FNB(X) = INT(40*RND(X)+1)
```

The characters available on the PET keyboard can be referred to by number. We will use the integers 1 to 250 to select the characters.

```
130 DEF FNC(X) = INT(250*RND(X)+1)
```

We will see how this number is used in a moment. In order to use the subroutine to position the cursor properly, we must first home the cursor. Then we can generate a row and column number, and call the subroutine.

```
140 PRINT "S"
150 R = FNA(X)
160 C = FNB(X)
170 GOSUB 400
```

Now we generate a character number and print the character using a new function, the CHR$ function.

```
180 N = FNC(X)
190 PRINT CHR$(N);
200 GOTO 140
```

Finally we have the subroutine to position the cursor.

```
400 REM SUBR TO POSITION CURSOR
410 FOR I = 1 TO R
420 PRINT "Q";
430 NEXT I
440 FOR J = 1 TO C
450 PRINT "J";
460 NEXT J
470 RETURN
```

The complete program follows.

```
100 X = 1
110 DEF FNA(X) = INT(25*RND(X)+1)
120 DEF FNB(X) = INT(40*RND(X)+1)
130 DEF FNC(X) = INT(250*RND(X)+1)
140 PRINT "S"
150 R = FNA(X)
160 C = FNB(X)
170 GOSUB 400
180 N = FNC(X)
190 PRINT CHR$(N);
200 GOTO 140
400 REM SUBR TO POSITION CURSOR
410 FOR I = 1 TO R
420 PRINT "Q";
430 NEXT I
440 FOR J = 1 TO C
450 PRINT "]";
460 NEXT J
470 RETURN
900 END
```

RUN this program and watch the screen display! You will have to press the STOP key to interrupt the program.

10-5 PROBLEMS

1. Write a program to generate and print out twenty-five random numbers of the form X.Y where X and Y are digits selected randomly from the set 0, 1, 2, ..., 9.

2. Write a program to generate and print out fifty integers selected at random from the range 13 to 25.

3. What will be printed out if the following program is executed?

```
100 FOR N =1 TO 20
110 PRINT INT(20*RND(1)+1)/100
120 NEXT N
130 END
```

4. If the following program is executed, what will be printed out?

```
100 FOR I = 1 TO 10
110 PRINT INT(100*RND(1))/10
120 NEXT I
130 END
```

5. Write a program that will simulate tossing a coin 10, 50, 100, 500, and 1000 times. In each case, print out the total number of heads and tails that occur.

6. Construct a dice-throwing simulation in BASIC. The dice are to be thrown twenty times. For each toss, print out the dice faces that are uppermost.

7. Write a program to generate and print out the average of 1000 random numbers selected from the range 0 to 1. What should this average be?

8. Modify the program of Example 3 and execute it as many times as needed to find the size of crowd such that there is a 50% chance that at least two people in the crowd have the same birthday.

9. John and Bill want to meet at the library. Each agrees to arrive at the library sometime between 1 and 2 P.M. They further agree that they will wait 10 minutes after arriving (but not after 2 P.M.), and if the other person has not arrived, will leave. Write a BASIC program to compute the probability that John and Bill will meet one another. Do a simulation of the problem using the random-number generator.

10. Suppose a bucket contains colored golf balls. There are ten red balls, five blue, two green, and eleven yellow. Write a BASIC program to simulate drawing five balls at random from the bucket if they are not replaced after being drawn. The printout should be the colors of the balls drawn in sequence.

11. Use the rule given in the discussion section in this chapter to generate and print out twenty-five numbers selected at random from a bell curve distribution of numbers with mean 10 and standard deviation 2. Round off the numbers to two places past the decimal point.

10-6 PRACTICE TEST

Take the following test to see how you are progressing. The answers are given at the end of the book.

1. Write a BASIC program to generate and print out 100 random integers selected from the set 1,2,3, and 4.

2. Write a BASIC program to generate and print out 100 random numbers over the range 25 to 50.

3. What will be printed out if we execute the following program?

```
100 FOR I = 1 TO 10
110 N = INT(2*RND(1)+1)
120 IF N = 1 THEN 150
130 PRINT "WHITE"
140 GOTO 160
150 PRINT "RED"
160 NEXT I
170 END
```

4. What will be printed out if we execute the following program?

```
100 FOR J = 1 TO 5
110 PRINT INT(1000*RND(1))/100
120 NEXT J
130 END
```

SOLUTIONS TO PRACTICE TESTS

Chapter 2

1. Press the RETURN key.

2. Turn PET off and then back on.

3. Multiplication is indicated by the * symbol.

4. Hold the SHIFT key down and press the CLR key.

5. Division.

6. PET will print out 2.

7. PET will print out "25+12/4".

8. Two characters will be deleted. The first is at the cursor position when DEL is pressed; the second is the character on the left. All the material on the right will be shifted left two characters.

Chapter 3

1. Press the RETURN key.

2. Press the RETURN key.

3. Press the STOP key.

4. There is no line number for the PRINT statement.

5. It is a clear indication that the program is complete and not a fragment of some other program.

6. Type the line number and press the RETURN key. Then redisplay the program.

7. Type it in using a line number not already in use.

8. Retype the line using the replacement information.

9. Type LIST.

10. Hold the SHIFT key down and press the CLR key.

11. Type NEW.

12. Type RUN.

13. Two letters or a letter followed by a single digit. Actually, you can be more general than this but it is best to stick to this notation.

14. The same as for question 13 except a $ character is tacked on the end.

Chapter 4

1. $-, *, +, \uparrow, /$

2. Exponentiation is done first; then multiplication and division. The last operations are addition and subtraction.

3. Left to right.

4. $\qquad$ 100 A = (4+3*B/D)↑2

5. The number 4.

6. (a) 5.67E+11 (b) 3.81E-06

7. (a) 7258000 (b) 0.001437

8. Division, addition, and exponentiation.

9. Place a tape in the cassette unit. Type SAVE "(the name of the program)" and then follow the instructions printed out on the screen.

10. Rewind the tape and type LOAD "(the name of the program)" and then follow the instructions printed on the screen.

Chapter 5

1. The numbers 1, 2, 3, 4, ... , and so on.

2. Assignment, INPUT, and READ DATA statements.

3. A character-string.

4. To put information into a program for the benefit of the reader. REM statements are ignored by the computer.

5. A DATA statement.

6. PET will print out "Y = 3".

7. Four.

8. As many as you want.

9. To provide for any spacing you want across the line.

10. PET will print the numbers 1 and 3 spaced in the standard column format, then on the next line, the numbers 1 and 3 will be printed spaced closer together.

11. PET will print out the message EXTRA IGNORED and the number 22.

12.
```
100 PRINT "HOW MANY MILES";
110 INPUT M
120 K = M*1.609
130 PRINT M;"MILES IS THE"
140 PRINT "SAME AS";K;"KM."
150 END
```

Chapter 6

1.
```
6
10
14
18
```

2.
```
BEST

BETTER
BEST

GOOD
BETTER
BEST
```

3.
```
100 PRINT "HOW MANY WIDGETS";
110 INPUT N
120 IF N <= 20 THEN 160
130 IF N <= 50 THEN 180
140 C = 1.5
150 GOTO 190
160 C = 2.
170 GOTO 190
180 C = 1.8
190 P = N*C
200 PRINT "PRICE PER WIDGET IS";C
210 PRINT "TOTAL COST OF ORDER IS";P
220 GOTO 100
230 END
```

4.
```
100 X = 0
110 PRINT X,
120 X = X+5
130 IF X <= 115 THEN 110
140 END
```

5.
```
100 PRINT "SPEED LIMIT";
110 INPUT L
120 PRINT "SPEED ARRESTED AT";
130 INPUT A
140 E = A-L
150 IF E <= 10 THEN 210
160 IF E <= 20 THEN 230
170 IF E <= 30 THEN 250
180 IF E <= 40 THEN 270
190 F = 80
200 GOTO 280
210 F = 5
220 GOTO 280
230 F = 10
240 GOTO 280
250 F = 20
260 GOTO 280
270 F = 40
280 PRINT "FINE IS";F;"DOLLARS"
290 END
```

Chapter 7

1.

20	18	16	14
12	10	8	6
4	2		

2. The numbers 1, 2, 3, 2, 4, 6, 3, 6, 9, 4, 8, 12 spaced vertically down the page.

3. 6, 7, 22.8, −1

4. Crossed loops.

5.
```
100 PRINT "MILES","KILOMETERS"
110 PRINT
120 FOR M = 10 TO 100 STEP 5
130 PRINT M,1.609*M
140 NEXT M
150 END
```

6.
```
100 DATA 10
110 DATA 25,21,24,21,26,27,25,24,23,24
120 READ N
130 S = 0
140 FOR I = 1 TO N
150 READ X
160 S = S+X
170 NEXT I
180 PRINT S/N
190 END
```

Chapter 8

1. To reserve space for an array and to tell the computer how big the array is.

2. X(3,4)

3. PET will print out "BILL 183".

4.
```
100 INPUT N
110 S = 0
120 FOR I = 1 TO N
130 INPUT X
140 IF X < 0 THEN 160
150 S = S+X
160 NEXT I
170 PRINT S
180 END
```

5. X$(2,4)

6.
```
100 DIM X(4,6)
110 FOR R = 1 TO 4
120 FOR C = 1 TO 6
130 X(R,C) = 4
140 NEXT C
150 NEXT R
160 FOR R = 1 TO 4
170 FOR C = 1 TO 6
180 PRINT X(R,C);
190 NEXT C
200 PRINT
210 NEXT R
220 END
```

7.
```
2      0      0      0      0

0      2      0      0      0

0      0      2      0      0

0      0      0      2      0

0      0      0      0      2
```

8. (a) DIM A(2,3) (b) 4 (c) 3 (d) 3

Chapter 9

1. (a) 4 (b) 14 (c) 30 (d) 80

2. The numbers 2, 1, 3, and 4.

3. (a) GOSUB (b) RETURN (c) to keep the program from falling into the subroutines.

4. The words WHITE, RED, and BLUE.

Chapter 10

1.
```
100 FOR I = 1 TO 100
110 PRINT INT(4*RND(1)+1)
120 NEXT I
130 END
```

2.
```
100 FOR I = 1 TO 100
110 PRINT 25+25*RND(1)
120 NEXT I
130 END
```

3. Ten words selected at random from the pair WHITE and RED.

4. Five numbers of the form X.YZ where X, Y, and Z are random digits.

SOLUTIONS TO ODD-NUMBERED PROBLEMS

Chapter 5

1.
```
100 CHAP 5, PROB 1
110 READ A,B,C,D
120 DATA 10,9,1,2
130 S = A+B
140 P = C*D
150 PRINT S,P
160 END
```

3.
```
        13      25
```

5.
```
100 REM CHAP 5, PROB 5
110 PRINT "TIME OF FALL (SEC)";
120 INPUT T
130 S = 16*T*T
140 PRINT "OBJECT FALLS";S;"FEET"
150 END
```

7.
```
100 INPUT A,B
110 C = A
120 A = B
130 B = C
140 PRINT A,B
150 END
```

9.
```
100 REM CHAP 5, PROB 9
110 PRINT "PRINCIPAL";
120 INPUT P
130 PRINT "INT. RATE (%)";
140 INPUT I
150 PRINT "TERM (YEARS)";
160 INPUT N
170 T = P*(1+I/100)↑N
180 PRINT "TOTAL VALUE IS";T
190 END
```

Chapter 6

1.
```
100 REM CHAP 6, PROB 1
110 INPUT X,Y
120 IF X > Y THEN 150
130 PRINT Y
140 GOTO 160
150 PRINT X
160 END
```

3.
```
100 REM CHAP 6, PROB 3
110 S = 0
120 X = 1
130 S = S+X
140 X = X+1
150 IF X <= 100 THEN 130
160 PRINT S
170 END
```

5.
```
OUT OF DATA ERROR IN LINE 130
```

7.
```
100 REM CHAP 6, PROB 7
110 S = 0
120 READ X
130 IF X = 9999 THEN 180
140 IF X < -10 THEN 120
150 IF X > 10 THEN 120
160 S = S+X
170 GOTO 120
180 PRINT S
190 DATA -1,22,17,-6,4,7,9999
200 END
```

9.
```
100 REM CHAP 6, PROB 9
110 INPUT A,B
120 IF A >= 10 THEN 130
121 GOTO 150
130 IF B >= 10 THEN 140
131 GOTO 150
140 PRINT A+B
141 GOTO 210
150 IF A < 10 THEN 160
```

```
151 GOTO 180
160 IF B < 10 THEN 170
161 GOTO 180
170 PRINT A*B
171 GOTO 210
180 IF A < B THEN 200
190 PRINT A-B
191 GOTO 210
200 PRINT B-A
210 END
```

11.
```
100 REM CHAP 6, PROB 11
110 PRINT "GROWTH RATE";
120 INPUT R
130 N = 0
140 Q = 1
150 Q = Q*(1+R/100)
160 N = N+1
170 IF Q <= 2 THEN 150
180 PRINT "NUMBER OF GROWTH PERIODS"
190 PRINT "TO DOUBLE IS";N
200 END
```

Chapter 7

1.
```
100 REM CHAP 7, PROB 1
110 PRINT "N","SQR(N)"
120 PRINT
130 FOR N = 2 TO 4 STEP .1
140 PRINT N,SQR(N)
150 NEXT N
160 END
```

3.
```
100 REM CHAP 7, PROB 3
110 INPUT N
120 FOR X = 0 TO N STEP 2
130 PRINT X
140 NEXT X
150 END
```

5.
```
                        0
                       -1
                        8
                        0
                        0
```

7.
```
        100 REM CHAP 7, PROB 7
        110 P = 1
        120 INPUT N
        130 FOR X = 1 TO N
        140 P = P*X
        150 NEXT X
        160 PRINT P
        170 END
```

9. Crossed X and Z loops.

11.
```
        100 REM CHAP 7, PROB 11
        110 PRINT "ANNUAL INVESTMENT";
        120 INPUT I
        130 PRINT "INTEREST RATE (%)";
        140 INPUT R
        150 PRINT "HOW MANY YEARS";
        160 INPUT N
        170 P1 = I
        180 FOR X = 1 TO N
        190 P2 = (P1+I)*(1+R/100)
        200 P1 = P2
        210 NEXT X
        220 PRINT "AT THE END OF THE"
        230 PRINT "LAST YEAR, THE VALUE"
        240 PRINT "OF THE INVESTMENT"
        250 PRINT "WILL BE";P1
        260 END
```

13.
```
        100 REM CHAP 7, PROB 13
        110 READ N
        120 PRINT "STUDENT","WTD GRADE"
        130 PRINT
        140 FOR I = 1 TO N
        150 READ M,X,Y,Z
        160 G = .25(X+Y)+.5*Z
        170 PRINT M,G
```

```
180 NEXT I
190 DATA 6
200 DATA 3,90,85,82
201 DATA 1,75,80,81
202 DATA 6,100,82,81
203 DATA 5,40,55,43
204 DATA 2,60,71,68
205 DATA 4,38,47,42
210 END
```

Chapter 8

1.
```
100 REM CHAP 8, PROB 1
110 DIM X(20)
120 READ N
130 FOR I = 1 TO N
140 READ X(I)
150 NEXT I
160 FOR I = 1 TO N
170 PRINT X(I)
180 NEXT I
190 DATA 12
200 DATA 2,1,4,3,2,4,5,6,3,5,4,1
210 END
```

3.   10

5.
```
100 REM CHAP 7, PROB 5
110 DIM X(100)
120 INPUT N
130 FOR I = 1 TO N
132 INPUT X(I)
134 NEXT I
140 FOR I = 1 TO N-1
150 IF X(I+1) < X(I) THEN 200
160 T = X(I+1)
170 X(I+1) = X(I)
180 X(I) = T
190 GOTO 140
200 NEXT I
210 FOR I = 1 TO N
212 PRINT X(I)
214 NEXT I
220 END
```

7.

1	1	1	1	1	1
0	0	0	0	0	0
0	0	1	1	1	1
0	0	0	0	0	0
0	0	0	0	1	1
0	0	0	0	0	0

9.

```
100 REM CHAP 8, PROB 9
110 DIM X(2,5)
120 FOR R = 1 TO 2
130 FOR C = 1 TO 5
140 READ X(R,C)
150 NEXT C
160 NEXT R
170 FOR R = 1 TO 2
180 FOR C = 1 TO 5
190 PRINT X(R,C);
200 NEXT C
210 PRINT
220 NEXT R
230 DATA 2,1,0,5,1
240 DATA 3,2,1,3,1
250 END
```

11.

```
100 REM CHAP 8, PROB 11
110 DIM X(20,20)
120 INPUT M,N
130 FOR R = 1 TO M
131 FOR C = 1 TO N
132 INPUT X(R,C)
133 NEXT C
134 NEXT R
140 FOR R = 1 TO M
150 S = 0
160 FOR C = 1 TO N
170 S = S+X(R,C)
180 NEXT C
190 PRINT "SUM OF ROW";R;"IS";S
200 NEXT R
210 FOR C = 1 TO N
220 P = 1
```

```
230 FOR R = 1 TO M
240 P = P*X(R,C)
250 NEXT R
260 PRINT "PRODUCT OF COLUMN";C;"IS";P
270 NEXT C
280 END
```

13.
```
100 REM CHAP 8, PROB 13
110 DIM X(4,6)
120 FOR R = 1 TO 4
121 FOR C = 1 TO 6
122 READ X(R,C)
123 NEXT C
124 NEXT R
130 DATA 48,40,73,120,100,90
140 DATA 75,130,90,140,110,85
150 DATA 50,72,140,125,106,92
160 DATA 108,75,92,152,91,87
170 FOR C = 1 TO 6
180 S = 0
190 FOR R = 1 TO 4
200 S = S+X(R,C)
210 NEXT R
220 PRINT "TOTAL - DAY";C;"IS";S
230 NEXT C
235 PRINT
240 FOR R = 1 TO 4
250 S = 0
260 FOR C = 1 TO 6
270 S = S+X(R,C)
280 NEXT C
290 PRINT "TOTAL - SALESPERSON";R;"IS";S
300 NEXT R
310 S = 0
320 FOR R = 1 TO 4
330 FOR C = 1 TO 6
340 S = S+X(R,C)
350 NEXT C
360 NEXT R
365 PRINT
370 PRINT "TOTAL SALES IS";S
380 END
```

15.
```
100 REM, CHAP 8, PROB 15
110 DIM X(20),A$(20)
120 INPUT N
130 FOR I = 1 TO N
140 INPUT A$(I),X(I)
```

```
150 NEXT I
160 FOR I = 1 TO N-1
170 IF X(I+1) < X(I) THEN 250
180 T = X(I+1)
190 T$ = A$(I+1)
200 X(I+1) = X(I)
210 A$(I+1) = A$(I)
220 X(I) = T
230 A$(I) = T$
240 GOTO 160
250 NEXT I
260 FOR I = 1 TO N
270 PRINT X(I),A$(I)
280 NEXT I
290 END
```

Chapter 9

1.
```
          25        5         20
          65
```

3.
```
     2        7        1        3        3
     7        10       3        3        3
     10       3        3        3        8
```

5.
```
     800 REM SUBR
     810 READ Z(1)
     820 T = 0
     830 FOR I = 2 TO 1+Z(1)
     840 T = T+Z(I)
     850 NEXT I
     860 RETURN
```

7.
```
     1000 REM SUBR
     1010 FOR I = 1 TO 45
     1020 PRINT "(HEART GRAPHIC CHAR.";
     1030 NEXT I
     1040 RETURN
```

Chapter 10

1.
```
100 REM CHAP 10, PROB 1
110 FOR I = 1 TO 25
120 N = INT(100*RND(1))/10
130 PRINT N,
140 NEXT I
150 END
```

3. Twenty random numbers of the form 0.XY.

5.
```
100 REM CHAP 10, PROB 5
110 FOR I = 1 TO 5
120 READ N
130 H = 0
140 T = 0
150 FOR J = 1 TO N
160 X = INT(2*RND(1)+1)
170 IF X = 1 THEN 200
180 T = T+1
190 GOTO 210
200 H = H+1
210 NEXT J
220 PRINT
230 PRINT "FOR";N;"TOSSES";
240 PRINT H;"HEADS";T;"TAILS"
250 NEXT I
260 DATA 10,50,100,500,1000
270 END
```

7.
```
100 REM CHAP 10, PROB 7
110 S = 0
120 FOR I = 1 TO 1000
130 S = S+RND(1)
140 NEXT I
150 PRINT S/1000
160 END
```

9.
```
100 REM CHAP 10, PROB 9
110 M = 0
120 FOR I = 1 TO 1000
130 A = 60*RND(1)
140 B = 60*RND(1)
150 IF ABS(A-B) > 10 THEN 170
160 M = M+1
170 NEXT I
```

```
180 PRINT "PROB. OF MEET IS";M/1000
190 END
```

11.
```
100 REM CHAP 10, PROB 11
110 FOR I = 1 TO 25
120 S = 0
130 FOR J = 1 TO 12
140 S = S+RND(1)
150 NEXT J
160 R = 10+2*(S-6)
170 PRINT INT(100*R+.5)/100
180 NEXT I
190 END
```

INDEX